What

Won't Tell You About

SEX, LOVE
and DATING

Greg Johnson
& Susie Shellenberger

What
HOLLYWOOD
Won't Tell You About
SEX, LOVE
and DATING

Greg
Johnson
&
Susie
Shellenberger

Regal Books
A Division of Gospel Light
Ventura, California, U.S.A.

Published by Regal Books
A Division of Gospel Light
Ventura, California, U.S.A.
Printed in U.S.A.

Regal Books is a ministry of Gospel Light, an evangelical Christian publisher dedicated to serving the local church. We believe God's vision for Gospel Light is to
provide church leaders with biblical, user-friendly materials that will help them
evangelize, disciple and minister to children, youth and families.

It is our prayer that this Regal Book will help you discover biblical truth for your
own life and help you meet the needs of others. May God richly bless you.

For a free catalog of resources from Regal Books/Gospel Light please contact your
Christian supplier or call 1-800-4-GOSPEL.

Cover design by Barbara Fisher.
Interior design by Britt Rocchio.

Library of Congress Cataloging-in-Publication Data
Johnson, Greg, 1956-
        What Hollywood won't tell you about sex, love and dating / Greg Johnson
and Susie Shellenberger.
        p. cm.
        ISBN 0-8307-1677-7
        1. Sexual ethics for teenagers—Juvenile literature. 2. Interpersonal rela-
tions in adolescence—Juvenile literature. 3. Dating (Social customs)—Religious
aspects—Christianity—Juvenile literature. 4. Interpersonal relations—Religious
aspects—Christianity—Juvenile literature. [1. Sexual ethics. 2. Interpersonal relations. 3. Dating (Social customs). 4. Christian life.] I. Shellenberger, Susie. II.
Title.
        HQ35.J58 1994   94-18277
        306.7'0835—dc20   CIP   AC

1 2 3 4 5 6 7 8 9 10 11 12 13 14 15 / 99 98 97 96 95 94 93

Rights for publishing this book in other languages are contracted by Gospel Literature
International (GLINT). GLINT also provides technical help for the adaptation, trans-
lation and publishing of Bible study resources and books in scores of languages
worldwide. For further information, contact GLINT, P.O. Box 4060, Ontario, CA
91761-1003, U.S.A., or the publisher.

Dedicated to my favorite guys in the world—Scott, Brett and Matt Shellenberger—who consistently strive for God's best. I admire your desire to be all He wants you to be.

- Susie

To the young men and women who are already committed to God's best in all of their relationships.

To those who have made mistakes and who now want to start afresh.

To those readers who will choose to remain pure because they read this book.

- GREG

Here's Some of the Stuff in This Book

✓ PART IV: SEX

✓ PART V: TOUGH ISSUES

PART 1

Intro Stuff
Personal Stories
A Few Words on Friendship

When We Left You Last...

GREG: Just in case you didn't get a chance to read our first book on guy/girl relationships (*Getting Ready for the Guy/Girl Thing,* and if you didn't read it—shame!), let's do a quick review on just how superior guys are.

1. We're stronger;
2. Less moody;
3. More communicative than girls—iftheywould-justletusgetawordinonceinawhile;
4. Better students (OK, scratch that one.);
5. Much better athl—

Susie: Greg! Are you trying to start this book without me?

GREG: Oh, hi, Susie. I didn't see you come in. Starting the book? Well, I was just trying to remind the guy reader-type person who has our book in his hands what our last book was about. I was just telling him some important facts he should always remember when relating to the opposite sex.

Susie: Yeah, I can see what you've done. Greg, how are we ever going to clear up the misconceptions guys have about dating, relating, love and sex if all you do is say stuff they want to hear?

GREG: But—

Susie: Don't you want guys to know that real success with the opposite sex isn't trying to be superior, but being respectful, sensitive and sticking to a high standard when they're around us girls who have been scientifically proven to be much better listeners, incredibly sensitive, caring, unselfish and more intelligent than any guy WHO'S EVER WALKED THE FACE OF THIS PLANET?

GREG: You're right, you're right. I see the point you're trying to make. I suppose we shouldn't just take the easy way and reinforce all the myths about how guys and girls should be dating and relating. After all, we didn't do that in our first book.

Susie: That's right, we really tried to bust the mold. We didn't just want guys and gals to have a few years of success with the opposite sex; we wanted them to have a *lifetime* of success. And what did we say?

GREG: Hey, nice transition.

Susie: Thanks.

GREG: We said the most important thing wasn't to try to go for the low-end goal of being popular with the opposite sex during the teen years, but to look at the BIG PICTURE. If teens want to be average during junior high and high school, then they should do what everyone else seems to be doing—forget God's values, think that your parents don't have a clue what hormones are, and, above all, don't respect yourself or the other person enough to keep your hands to yourself.

What else did we try to say, Susie?

Susie: Ooo, nice lead-in.

GREG: Hey, thanks.

Susie: We also said that because God made them—and actually died on a cross for them—He probably has a few things to say about what real success with the opposite sex looks like. We reminded them how much power He has for those who call for help, how forgiving He is to anyone who has already made mistakes, and how incredibly patient and understanding He is with followers who want a lifetime of success, instead of a lifetime of regrets.

GREG: You know, Susie, that word "regret" is pretty powerful.

Susie: How so?

GREG: I hate to regret things. To look back and think, *I was a lamebrain for treating that person like an object. I was a knuckleface—*

Susie: That's knucklehead.

GREG: Right, a knuckleheadface *for not realizing that what I did could have lifelong consequences, not only for me, but also for any future children I might want, or any future spouse.*

I think I speak for both of us, Susie, when I say the best thing Christian guys or gals can do is to examine what they really want in life as it relates to the opposite sex and then not let anything stand in their way, especially when it's something this important.

Susie: Greg, because this is a book, and two people can't have their fingers on the computer keys at once (or else it looks like "aldnfgpoi whtqo-hwer[0189 4hjdslf vldsf nODif jhioq[op' alsdjfJF'L KMFGLNMA"), you *can* say that for me.

You sound as though you know from a bad experience that not having your mind in the right gear can really cause you to do things you shouldn't. Is that personal experience, Greg?

GREG: Yikes, was it that obvious?

Susie: Though you're OLDER than I am, Greg, it's not as if you were a teenager growing up in the '60s. You remember what it was like to be young and in love. I think a good place to start this book would be for you to talk about all of your juicy failures. Although you married your high school sweetheart, you guys didn't always make the right choices, right?

GREG: Right, Susie. But I don't think the person reading this book would be THAT interested in hearing about all of my failures. They probably want to hear that I finally have my act together when it comes to females; that I'm a Christian now.

Susie: You're sweet, and modest, but wrong, Greg!

GREG: OK. But for those who can't stand hearing about such things, skip to chapter 3.

I Was a Teenage Jerk

I (Greg) wasn't a Christian in high school. My life was sports, TV, friends and poker parties. My sophomore year, I fell in deep-like with a girl. Though I didn't think I'd marry her, it sure felt good to have a girlfriend. But after three months together, she dumped me. Obviously, THE GIRL had a problem!

I was crushed! I remember just vegging out in my room, listening to music for hours on end. What do you think was going through my mind? *How could she do this to me?* Now I was left to try to find another girlfriend. After all, guys have to either be talking about someone, pursuing someone or going with someone, right? (Wrong! But we'll talk about this one later.)

My senior year approached, and I vowed to forget about girls until after basketball season.

I broke that vow during football season as soon as I discovered that a girl named Danielle would go out with me if I asked her. She had nice eyes, so I thought I should at least ask. Well, we dated for a few weeks, but something was different about her. I soon found out she was a Christian. I knew that meant she would hardly let me kiss her, let alone touch her. She was attractive, but modest. She held her ground, and when I told her I wanted to break up, it was her who wound up crying, not me.

This girl stuff was getting weird. It was time for another vow. This time, *definitely* no girls until after basketball!

About a week later, I heard through the grapevine (you know, the blonde girl in every school who knows who likes whom before anyone else) that a girl named Elaine liked me. We were friends, but I'd never considered her for a girlfriend. (At least not until after basketball.)

But then something happened, something that most of my friends only dreamed about: She actually told me she liked me!

"After basketball, Babe," I said. (As though that kind of thing happened to me every day.)

I couldn't hold out. But I did wait a whole week before breaking down and asking her if she wanted to get something to eat after my game on Friday. I was unattached, she was cute and popular. I was insecure and hated to ask girls out on dates (for fear of rejection, naturally). Also, I wasn't that popular, so this was all very intriguing. I had a way to have a girlfriend without all the usual nerve-racking routines.

We immediately jumped into a dating relationship. That is, we weren't interested in being interested in anyone else besides each other. She was a Christian (*Why did I keep getting stuck with Christian girlfriends?*), and after our first real date she told me she would never marry someone who wasn't a Christian. Not knowing what that meant—and not being too interested in marriage at the time—that statement didn't mean much to me.

I've learned through the years that someone with bad morals usually pulls down someone with good morals, not vice versa. Because I wasn't committed to staying a virgin until marriage, I, naturally, tried to do all I could to pull

Elaine down. She held strong for a while, but eventually allowed some exploring. Physical excitement led both of us to believe we were in love. We liked each other, but neither of us had any clue what committed Christian love was all about—especially me.

We continued dating for nine months before she finally had the spiritual maturity to confront me about where I was putting my hands. She knew she could have lost me, but still had the courage to risk that in order to regain the ground she had given up. I faced a crisis, too. She was growing in her faith, and I wasn't a Christian. Unless I became one, I was certain we would be finished.

The short ending of this story is that I *did* become a Christian, but not for fear of losing Elaine. I finally realized I needed God—for me. Two years later we were married. We're still married! 💙

Lessons in Stupidity

Fortunately, this story has a happy ending. But it sure had a rough beginning. Even though Elaine was a Christian, she allowed her faith to be compromised by her non-Christian boyfriend—me! Although we never had sex before we were married, we came close many times. Technically, we were sexually pure. But were we? I don't think so. While we wanted to do what was right, we didn't. In fact, 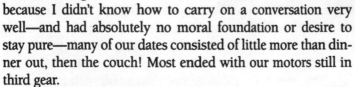 because I didn't know how to carry on a conversation very well—and had absolutely no moral foundation or desire to stay pure—many of our dates consisted of little more than dinner out, then the couch! Most ended with our motors still in third gear.

Physical contact led us to believe we were in love. The more physical we got, the more we thought we loved each other. It acted like a false glue. We were close, but it was an artificial closeness.

Up until our wedding, we always went farther than we

should have. Only Elaine's sheer determination—and my new, but wimpy, faith—kept us both virgins until the honeymoon.

What happened next? Everything went fine after that, right?

Sadly, no. What should have been the funnest time in our lives turned out to be 3 years of continued frustration. You see, I had trained Elaine's body to go to a certain point, then stop. (OK, she had a part in that training, but I was the real culprit.) When you do that for an extended period of time (as we did for 2 years), even though your mind, God and the world says sex is OK, your body is still programmed to stop. It took three years of hurt feelings, failure, rejection and selfish mistakes before her body got "reprogrammed." It was a terrible way to start a marriage. I would even go so far as to say it affected us for more than 10 years.

Here were our main mistakes:

• Elaine shouldn't have dated a nonbeliever who wasn't interested in learning more about the Christian faith. She was playing with fire, and it was only a miracle she didn't end up ruining her goal of remaining a virgin for her husband.

• Once Elaine saw I wasn't interested in talking (or didn't know how), she should have taught me how to converse—or dumped me. Trust me, you DON'T want a relationship with someone who can't or doesn't want to learn how to talk.

• After I became a Christian, we tried to set certain limits, but it was next to impossible to go back to the stage where we should have been. Each level we went through got old after a while, so we kept "progressing up." Because physical contact wasn't kept at levels that would keep us out of trouble, failure and frustration were the inevitable results.

The reason I wanted to open the book with my stupid mistakes is to let you know where I come from. Plus, I felt it would give you hope and help for the future. Many of you reading these pages have made similar mistakes—or worse. One thing I've learned:

YOU CAN *START RIGHT* OR *START OVER* RIGHT.

Do you want to do things right, beginning today? If so, this book is a good place to start. Why? Because Susie and I don't want you to be a dork around the opposite sex, so we're going to share some great stuff with you. We also don't want you to have to face the consequences of making mistakes, so we're going to tell you the truth. We're as committed as we can be to YOUR SUCCESS with the opposite sex.

And speaking of success, lest you think you're just going to hear from a guy who had to learn everything the hard way, I want Susie to talk about her dating life. So grab a tall glass of water and hear from a gal who has made a commitment to doing things right from her earliest teen years.

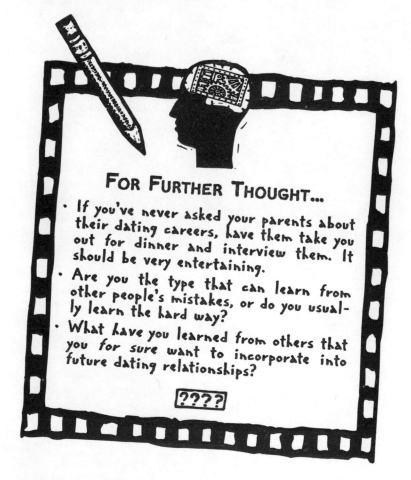

FOR FURTHER THOUGHT...

- If you've never asked your parents about their dating careers, have them take you out for dinner and interview them. It should be very entertaining.
- Are you the type that can learn from other people's mistakes, or do you usually learn the hard way?
- What have you learned from others that you for sure want to incorporate into future dating relationships?

????

A Great Start!

Though I (Susie) didn't realize it when I was a teen, I now know that I was really fortunate! I had the privilege of growing up in a Christian home with two parents who were crazy about me.

When it came to attending church, it wasn't an option. My brother and I didn't have a choice. If the church doors were open, we were there: Sunday morning, Sunday evening, Wednesday nights and anytime there was a revival or missionary service. But you know what? I loved it. Church was where exciting things happened.

I learned at church how incredible it was to walk each and every day with the Creator of the universe, and to be on a first-name basis with Him! It was there I realized that the same mighty power that set the stars in the sky and put the whole world in motion was *mine* to live by. No way would I miss that! Getting to know God deeper and better was too exciting!

We had a huge youth group that went on choir tours, mission trips, scavenger hunts and mystery outings. I was involved in discipleship groups, Bible studies, drama productions and, of course, our regular youth meetings.

MY DATING LIFE

You've probably already guessed that church is where I made my closest friendships. I had friends outside of church, and I enjoyed the 2,000-student public school I attended. But when it came to developing dating relationships, I chose to date boys from my youth group. *Why?* Because *these* were the guys I watched every week. I noticed their spiritual growth. I listened to what they had to share in youth group, and I watched their involvement in church. I could see the difference Christ was making in their lives.

Because I knew I'd never marry a non-Christian, I thought, *Why date one?* I was *friends* with non-Christian guys, but to me there was a huge difference in being friends with someone and establishing a closer relationship with him.

My standards were set, and I had been taught not to compromise. Now I know some of you are thinking, *Well, I don't have a huge youth group. There aren't very many guys at my church. And the ones who come aren't guys I want to go out with.*

Please don't think I'm being harsh, but, OK, here goes: Then what's wrong with *not* dating right now?

You're crazy! I'm in high school. I HAVE to date! you're probably saying.

Well, realistically, you don't *have* to. I mean, you won't keel over and die if you're not dating. You might *feel* as though you're gonna die, but dating really isn't the most important thing in the world. Your walk with God is.

I know, I know. Some of you who disagree are really ticked and wish you hadn't even bought this book. Tell you what. Close the pages, go grab a Diet Cherry 7-Up, come back and I'll leave a huge white space for you to doodle your feelings on, OK? After you've run out of ink, meet me on the next page.

DOODLE ZONE

Get busy.

What I'm saying is: **Don't date someone just to be dating someone.** If you do, chances are you'll compromise your standards. Be superselective and don't simply go out with anyone who asks. Some "Christian" guys are even more "handsy" than some non-Christian guys. So establish a reputation of being choosy.

Because Greg was honest about his dating experiences, I will be, too. I've never gone past a kiss. Maybe some of you are like me. You know what your standards are, and you're unwilling to compromise. GOOD JOB! I hope you don't feel intimidated when you hear others bragging about their sexual experiences.

So how have I kept such high standards? Well, several factors contributed. My relationship with Christ is the *most important* thing in my life. I'm going to do *nothing* to jeopardize that. My parents' influence and church involvement helped establish a strong sense that giving in was not God's best; seeing the big picture instead of a lifetime of success with the opposite sex was really what I wanted.

I'm still single—and still dating—and I've kept my standards high.

WHAT ABOUT YOU?

Maybe, like Greg, you've gone exploring physically with your dates. Or maybe, like me, you've never gone past a kiss. Maybe you're a sexually active teen or have had an abortion.

Wherever you are on the long scale of friendship, dating and sex, we're here for you. Will you let us give you our *hearts* through this book? In no way do we want you to perceive these pages as a finger-pointing lecture from people you really don't even want to listen to. We care.

If you think *that* sounds corny, you'll probably roll your eyes at *this* one: Will you stop right now, before going any farther in the book, and ask Christ to use it to make a difference in your dating life?

We don't think it's corny. In fact, we're praying the same thing *for* you.

> Jesus, I feel kinda funny praying right now, but here's the deal: I started reading this because I DO care about my dating life. I also care about my walk with You. Help me never to let a guy/girl become more important than You. Sometimes I need help in keeping You in the number one spot in my life. That's where I WANT You; now give me the strength to make that desire a reality.
>
> And, Lord, use this book to help me establish the right dating standards. I want to have godly dating relationships; I'm just not always sure how to do it.
>
> OK, I've asked for Your help. Now, I'm gonna keep reading. Please make the important stuff register in my heart and mind. I'll grab a pen so I can highlight anything I feel You want me to read twice.
>
> Amen.

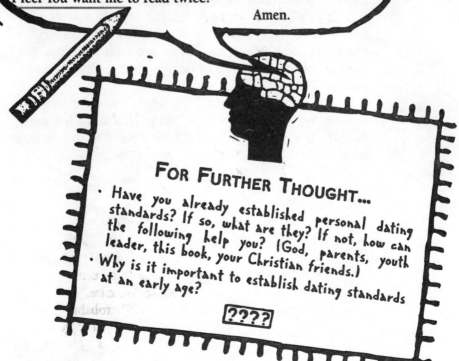

FOR FURTHER THOUGHT...

- Have you already established personal dating standards? If so, what are they? If not, how can the following help you? (God, parents, youth leader, this book, your Christian friends.)

- Why is it important to establish dating standards at an early age?

????

THE BEST PLAN FOR YOU

Are you ready for the guy/girl thing?

We asked that question a bunch of times in our first book. The reason: We don't think you should be in any hurry to start pairing up. Learning how to build strong friendships with the opposite sex is a far better plan than worrying about which girl to ask out this Friday or what guy to start pursuing.

But we know that many teens *do* want to relate, date and perhaps even "go with" someone. They're mature enough, their parents have given the OK and they don't mind facing the inevitable rejection that comes with being into dating.

This book is for those who...

...want to be ready to date.

...have already begun dating a little.

...have been into dating for a long time and want a few more good ideas on how to do it right.

If you like the opposite sex, but are still a ways away from wanting a one-on-one date or relationship with them—that's fine. Each person has his or her own time line. But don't force yourself to date or pair up just because a few others do.

The next section tackles the whole issue of dating and relating. We'll talk just to guys, just to girls and a few times to both. If a chapter doesn't interest you, skip to one that does.

PART II

Dating Stuff
First Date Ideas
Modesty and Respect
Parents and Dating

DATING STUFF:
GUYS ONLY!

4

What Girls Think About Guys...as Friends

Usually, a person of the opposite sex can make a fantastic friend, but beware: those ol' friendship feelings sometimes turn to affection! *Then* what's a guy to do? Moving from pals to sweethearts could be a roller-coaster encounter not worth taking the chance!

Do you need some heartfelt advice for tackling the issue of moving from friendship to romance? Here are six Southern belles to give you a bit of insight into the complex thoughts and emotions of a female.

HOW SHOULD GUYS START FRIENDSHIPS WITH GIRLS?

Jennifer: Begin with light, easy conversation about things you have in common, such as a class, teacher, church, parents, etc.

Kristin: Hang out at the same places she does and go to the same events. Also, have a mixed group of friends at school to do things together.

Hilangela: Just start up a conversation—but be sure she wants a friendship, too.

Alicia: If he just listens to her, that can get things off to a good start. Don't be afraid to ask her how things are in her life.

Laura: Try going out with a bunch of friends and asking a friend to bring her along.

We All Agree: A smart guy will find out what the girl likes to do and what she's interested in, then make it a point to talk to her about those things.

HOW SHOULD GUYS LET THEIR INTENTIONS BE KNOWN IF THEY WANT TO MOVE PAST THE FRIENDSHIP STAGE?

Hilangela: Just tell her.

Laura: Yeah, they should flat out say it!

Celeste: By making a point to talk to her and learn more about her. That way the transition won't be hard.

Alicia: The guy could say, "Look, I'm starting to have feelings for you beyond just friendship." Or he can send her a rose with a sweet little card that says basically the same thing.

Jennifer: He should call a lot and act more interested. The way he treats the girl will let her know.

Kristin: He should ask her out to a place away from your "group"—someplace very nice and different—then she'll know he thinks she's special.

Hey Greg:

When I'm around a girl I like, why do my hands and pits start to sweat? It's very embarrassing. —Oakridge, Oregon

GREG: The same thing probably happens right before a big game or a test in one of your classes. Your body is producing an adrenalin rush. The hormone epinephrine is being activated in your system to prepare the body for what the brain has communicated is important. It's a lot like getting butterflies in the stomach. That occurs when the blood rushes from your intestinal area (where it helps digest things) to your muscles so you'll have more strength for the upcoming task.

Sweat and butterflies are normal. There's nothing you can do about it until your mind begins telling your hormones the situation is no big deal. The only way that can happen is through continual practice.

◀ AT WHAT POINT DOES A GUY SEEM ▶ OBNOXIOUS WHEN HE'S TRYING TO ▶ GET A GIRL TO NOTICE HIM?

Celeste: When he does something stupid that, in his better judgment, he wouldn't have done.

Kristin: Yeah, like when he starts acting silly and goofy, trying desperately to show off his manliness. He needs to know when to go away!

Laura: It drives me crazy when a guy calls every day and has nothing to say!

Alicia: A guy is obnoxious when he aggravates and bugs a girl until she finally goes out with him. But that's *not* the way to get a girl to like him.

Jennifer: When he acts like a tough guy in front of his friends; he's just puttin' on a show, trying to impress her.

Hilangela: When he follows her around!

We All Agree: Guys get obnoxious when they give you so much attention that all your friends are teasing you! He should just relax and be himself.

▶ HOW CAN A GUY KNOW IF THE ◀ ▶ GIRL JUST WANTS TO STAY FRIENDS? ◀

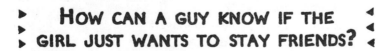

Alicia: If she goes on and on about how busy she is and has no time for social life, that's an obvious clue. Plus, if she says she doesn't want to jeopardize their friendship by getting romantically involved, he should believe her.

Kristin: When the girl starts dating someone else, he can be sure she's not interested in more than a friendship with him.

Hilangela: By the way she acts.

Celeste: That's right. The girl will make it clear by keeping her distance for a while.

Jennifer: He'll know by her bored tone of voice and the fact that she'll definitely not flirt with him. If he tries to hold her hand or put his arm around her, she'll stiffen up or pull away.

HOW LONG SHOULD A GUY BE FRIENDS WITH YOU BEFORE HE ACTS INTERESTED?

Celeste: Long enough to get to know me so I can be sure the attraction won't be based on appearance only.

Kristin: We need to be friends for a minimum of two months before he acts interested.

Alicia: I agree. That way, I'd have more than enough time to get to know him and find out his good and bad qualities.

Jennifer: I don't think there should be a specific time limit. But you do at least need to find out if the guy has a decent reputation.

Laura: Three weeks—no longer!

Hilangela: At least one week!

WHAT ABOUT THE OLD "TELL YOUR BEST FRIEND TO TELL HER BEST FRIEND TO TELL HER THAT HE LIKES HER" ROUTINE? WHAT OTHER "SAFE" OPTIONS DO GUYS HAVE WITHOUT FEELING TOTALLY REJECTED?

Kristin: The only way the guy won't feel totally reject-ed is to get to know a girl well enough so that he can pretty much predict her answer.

Celeste: The girl can help keep a guy from feeling total-ly rejected with a sweet, kind refusal that doesn't leave him feeling worthless.

Jennifer: If a guy decides to tell a friend to tell a friend to tell a friend, you can count on the message get-ting mixed up and lots of hurt feelings later. Maybe he could write her a letter.

Laura: If the girl seems to enjoy spending time with him, she'll most probably go out with him. So be casual and see what happens.

Hilangela: The guy could try hinting without being overly obvious.

Alicia: Telling him through a friend that you're not interested is a safe way, but it's indirect.

We All Agree: Dating isn't "safe" and there is always a chance of rejection, but you have to take the risk!

Hey Greg:
How do you tell a girl she has something in her teeth?
—Toronto, Canada

GREG: I like the direct approach:
"Excuse me. I wouldn't say this to anyone, but you have a large piece of spinach between your number one and two incisors."
Or...

"If it wasn't for that red pepper completely covering your lowers, you'd have a gorgeous smile."

Or, if you like the subtle approach:

"I hate to ask this, but do I have anything in *my* teeth?" (Hopefully, she'll get the hint and return the question.)

Or...

"I know we hardly know each other, but this is something I ask all my dates. When you have something in your teeth, do you like it or hate it when the guy points it out?"

FLOSS

MOST GIRLS ARE TOO NICE TO TELL A BOY STRAIGHT-OUT SHE'S NOT INTERESTED, BUT WHAT CLUES SHOULD A GUY PICK UP?

Laura: If she's always too busy, he needs to face the facts!

Kristin: Some guys are clueless, but when a girl always makes excuses, it's obvious she does *not* want to go out with him.

Hilangela: If the girl doesn't talk to him, he should get the hint!

Celeste: When the girl quietly avoids him or laughs off his advances, it should be a good signal.

Alicia: Talking about guys she likes, dating other guys and purposely dodging him whenever possible are sure clues!

Jennifer: Some obvious clues would be when she refuses to take his calls, or she turns and goes the other way when she sees him coming down the hall at school! Another big one is when she avoids having eye contact with him.

✳

By Andrea Stephens, who is the fashion editor for *Brio* magazine and lives in Covington, La. This article first appeared in the October 1993 issue of *Breakaway*.

FOR FURTHER THOUGHT...

• Guys, what did you learn from this chapter? Do girls seem more approachable now? Why or why not?

• Girls, what advice, if any, would you change? What advice would you add?

• Guys, what do you wish girls understood better about you?

• Girls, what do you wish you understood better about guys?

????

The Right Age to Date

The Bible says the right age to date is...
Josh McDowell says the right age to date is...
Dr. Dobson says the right age to date is...
Your parents say the right age to date is...

Hey, it doesn't matter to us what any of these authorities has to say!

Why?

Well, the Bible doesn't talk about dating or courting. Josh and Dr. Dobson don't give ages and the real authority is your parents, anyway.

Naturally, though, we have a few things to say on the subject. How can you know when you're actually ready to be trusted alone (or semi-alone) with another person?

Here are two checklists, one for guys and one for girls, that we believe are the absolute minimums. If you can honestly say you meet or exceed each standard, you're probably ready to one-on-one date.

GUYS

I have transportation.

I'm not dating to increase my popularity.

I'm not dating to prove to a friend that I'm not afraid of girls.

I don't want to date in order to go "exploring" with a particular girl.

I realize that I probably won't marry the girl I'm dating, so I'd better treat her the way I would want a guy to treat the girl I WILL marry.

I'm dating to get to know a certain girl I'm attracted to.

I realize this girl is a unique creation of God and deserves to be treated with respect.

I really want to learn how to communicate better with girls.

GIRLS

I won't wear something suggestive in order to keep the guy's attention.

I won't succumb to the temptation to do something physical in order to keep the guy interested.

I'm not dating to boost my shaky feelings of self-worth; I don't need to date to realize I'm someone of value.

I won't date any guy I can't trust.

It's easy for me to speak my mind and say, "No, I'm not into that" if the guy gets physically pushy.

I'm just as content *not* dating (enjoying my friends and family) as I would be if I *were* involved in a relationship.

I really want to learn how to communicate better with guys.

FOR FURTHER THOUGHT...

- How can dating too early lead to trouble in later years?

- What do you think is an appropriate age for group dating? Single dating? Dating one person exclusively?

- Do any of the "minimum standards" listed above or in the chapter seem unreasonable to you? Why do you object? Can you see the value of the standard even though you disagree with it?

- If you've talked with your parents about dating, what have you concluded together about the right age to date?

????

FIRST DATE STUFF: GUYS ONLY!

It Doesn't Have to Be Worse than Asking Her Out

Guys, if you decide that a one-on-one date is a good idea with a certain girl, all of your problems aren't solved when she agrees to see you. No matter how shy you are, you have to learn the skill of talking to adults. Namely, her parents.

If you want to be chicken about it, you might be able to slink away without doing more than saying "hi." But that's a BIG mistake. Not only do her parents have a right to know more about you, you should want them to. A girl's parents who don't bother checking out the guys whom she dates:

1. Probably aren't too involved with her and let her do what she wants;
2. Don't care;
3. Might be cereal killers...I mean, serial killers!

All could be signs that the girl may not care about herself, either. You should appreciate the fact they're concerned enough about her to ask you a few questions.

So what will they ask? *(What are they REALLY looking for?)*

• What does your dad (or mom) do for a living? *(Does he have two parents at home?)*

• How did you two meet? *(Are you someone other adults might know, so I can check you out in case the relationship goes any further?)*

• Where are you off to? *(Is there a phone around she could use in case she needs to escape your hormones? Will there be other adults in the general vicinity? Does your route take you through any dangerous parts of town?)*

• What time do you think you'll be home? *(Are you a guy who keeps his word?)*

• What are your favorite subjects? What are you involved in outside of school? *(Is this guy a mental or social moron with his brains in his biceps?)*

If you think a parent doesn't have the right to know the answers to these questions, you need to retake Dating 101. Just be glad they don't ask about your thought life. (And if you're a girl reading this and you think you'll just die if your mom or dad asks your date these questions, get a life! Be extremely thankful your parents care enough about you to risk embarrassing you a little so they can make sure you'll be safe with this stranger.)

After you've looked her parents in the eye (hint, hint), stayed calm, talked slowly and clearly, and answered these questions, there are bonus points to be earned. Assuming you have the time (come early so you will), ask *them* a few questions:

• When did you two first meet? (Assuming that both her mom and dad are standing in front of you, and that she lives with both parents.)

• What do you do for a living? Do you like it?

• This is a nice house, where did you get that (fill in the

blank with "grandfather's clock," "piano"—something in the room that looks like it may have a story attached to it)?

• What do you like to do in your spare time, Mr. So-and-So? (Before you ask this one, make sure he has the same last name as the girl you're dating. That's not always the case.)

OPTIONAL:

• Can I tell you about my thought life?

• Would you like to hear how my dad got put into prison?

• How do I compare to the last guy who took out your daughter?

• Is that a toupee or your real hair?

• Your wife sure looks like she's a good cook. Does your daughter cook that well?

• Your daughter is the eighth girl I've dated this month. Want to know how I do it?

• Is it OK to bring your daughter back anytime between 11:00 and 1:00? I'm not sure when the movie is over.

• Would I be a total doofus if I asked any of these optional questions?

Hey Greg:

I want to get to know this girl in my English class. The problem is, she's not very popular and she's kinda plain looking. I know that if my friends found out I wanted to date her, they'd make fun of me for weeks. She's got such a great personality that I hate to pass up the chance to be closer friends. Any suggestions on how to handle my buddies? —Arlington, Texas

GREG: When I was in high school, I faced the exact same dilemma. There were dozens of great girls who weren't cheerleaders or popular, but they were great gals! The only thing that held me back was what I thought my friends would say.

Though I married my high school sweetheart and have never regretted it, here's what happens: After you graduate, you lose contact with practically ALL of those buddies who are so important to you now, so what they think in the long run really doesn't matter. Then, at your 5- and 10-year reunions, all the girls you thought were plain have "improved"—A LOT. Plus, most still have the great personality you were attracted to in the first place.

Don't let the fear of what your friends might say detour you from getting to know girls who are full of potential. The fact is, if your friends rip on you for dating these girls, they're probably just jealous because they didn't have the courage to ask them out themselves!

Now that you've answered her parents' questions and asked a few of your own, here are a few more things to remember:

1. Be a man who keeps his word. If you say you'll have her home by 10:00 P.M., that doesn't mean 10:05. That's the funny thing about parents who care: they also have a tendency to worry. Worried parents are not happy parents. They can't sleep until everything in their world is right. If you're late bringing their daughter home, things aren't right! When you know you're going to be late—even five minutes—YOU call her parents.

"Hello, Mr. Williams. Beth and I got caught in the checkout line at the bowling alley, trying to return our shoes. We're on our way right now, and should be there in 10 minutes. Is that OK?"

IS THAT OK?! He'll probably call you "son" when you get back! You've just shown him you'll accept responsibility, you're truthful and you're concerned about his feelings. (If he offers to buy the engagement ring, don't say no right away. Tell him you'll keep it in mind.)

2. You may be asked to give a full report when you bring her home. Don't do anything you may be tempted to lie about.

Though most guys drop off their dates and speed away,

don't be like most guys. If her parents are in bed, you don't have to wake them up, but don't be afraid to come in to make sure they know your eyes aren't bloodshot, and you can still walk a straight line. Tell them what you did before they ask. Thank them for letting you take their daughter out and wave good-bye.

3. When you get home (or the next day), debrief with your dad how the date went.

Though some dads might be too ignorant to care (because *their* dads probably never even talked to them about dating), make a point to break that mold. Ask your dad what you could have done differently or better. Being an open book with your dad in your relationships with girls has tons of benefits and no drawbacks.

> Following this advice on what to do before and after a date may make you feel good, but it probably won't beat having a great time ON THE DATE! Next up: Susie is going to talk to the girls on what makes a great first date.

GREG: Guys, have you ever thought about what your dad's hope is for you with the opposite sex?

Probably not.

Most guys think dads are out of touch—whatever struggles *they* faced aren't anything like *yours*. If you're not interested in your dad's perspective, feel free to skip this section. If you are, read on.

Dads are funny; they're hard to read sometimes. Besides teasing you, warning you, trying to coach you, or possibly ignoring you, most have some things they really want to communicate. I asked a few dads, and here's what they said:

TIPS FROM DADS

- "It's OK to make mistakes in the teenage years, but please don't get too wrapped up with one girl."
- "I want my son to be interested in girls, but I want him to learn sexual self-control before marriage (in dating)."

- "During the early teen years, don't spend months with the same girl. The important thing isn't to become emotionally attached but to practice relating to a wide variety of girls. You'll never know which kind of girl to settle down with if you only give yourself a few options."
- "Develop the character qualities necessary to be a good friend, not a good boyfriend."
- "Though I know it's tough and sometimes embarrassing for you, I really want to go through these days with you. I may not have all the answers, but I'll listen."
- "The best thing I can do for you is to tell you about the mistakes I made. Then at least you'll know whether you want to make the same mistakes or not."
- "If you get a girl pregnant or go too far physically and I find out, it *will* be tough for me to deal with. But God forgives you, so I can't do anything less. I'll always forgive you and stick by you."

GREG: How courageous are you? I realize not every guy has a great relationship with his dad (or even has a dad at home). So talking about *this* subject in particular may be awkward. But I want to challenge you to do the right—the courageous—thing: If you can say something like what is written below in your own words, say it. If not—and it expresses the desire of your heart—then simply read it. The goal is to get across an honest message.

Dad, you may or may not be aware that I've discovered the opposite sex. Not having gone through this before, I don't know everything to do or say when it comes to girls. I know that because I'm a teenager, it's my job to make mistakes, but this is one area I definitely don't want to fail in.

How comfortable are you in talking with me about this guy/girl thing? (Pause, wait for a response.)

Dad, here's what I need: First, I don't need to be

nagged or made fun of in front of Mom or the relatives. Second, there will probably be some secrets I'll keep. It'll be hard to tell you absolutely everything. Don't be offended, OK? Third, I don't need you to ask me questions all the time. How about if you say something like, "Time to talk?" when it's been awhile or you see me acting weird. I'll know what you mean, and I'll let you know.

What I *do* need is to hear what *you* did right and what *you* did wrong, a listening ear, some ideas, a little encouragement—and probably some forgiveness and grace when I make a mistake. I need from you what God gives me—unconditional love.

I'd like to keep you in the loop on my dating life as much as possible. Are you up for it, Dad?

If you don't have a dad at home to do this with, perhaps a neighbor, your youth leader or your coach will work, maybe even a grandpa. It's important that you have someone older to talk to. If you rely solely on the advice you get from friends, it won't be enough. In fact, in some cases, it will be like the blind leading the blind. Learning from the experience of a trusted adult is the key.

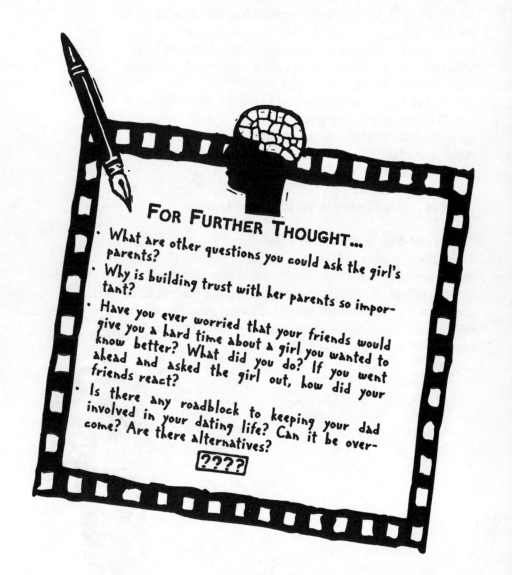

FOR FURTHER THOUGHT...

- What are other questions you could ask the girl's parents?
- Why is building trust with her parents so important?
- Have you ever worried that your friends would give you a hard time about a girl you wanted to know better? What did you do? If you went ahead and asked the girl out, how did your friends react?
- Is there any roadblock to keeping your dad involved in your dating life? Can it be overcome? Are there alternatives?

????

DATING STUFF:

GUYS AND GIRLS

7

So Little Time, So Many Choices

The size of the town you live in and size of the church you attend will determine how many dating choices you have. Some teens can look at a sea of datable faces; for others, the pickins are slim.

Whether you have 10 or 110 possibilities to choose from doesn't have to alter your reasons—or your standards—for whom to spend time with. Here are a few things to consider before you risk rejection and approach him/her for the first time.

FAITH

Is he/she a Christian? Is he/she open to discussing *your* religious beliefs?

The Bible doesn't specifically say to not date non-Christians. It says, "Do not be yoked together with unbelievers. For what do righteousness and wickedness have in common? Or what fellowship can light have with darkness?" (2 Cor. 6:14).

Though "yoked" is a word that implies much more than a simple date, it's better to be safe. Given the fact that our hearts can quickly become attached, don't, if at all possible, one-on-one date someone who doesn't share a similar belief in God and the authority of the Bible.

VALUES

Though we hear this complaint more from girls than guys these days, faith and values are two different things: *I'm dating a Christian, but he can't keep his hands off me. We're constantly going too far.*

Just because someone has faith in Christ doesn't mean that person values what God values. Many church-going Christians aren't convinced sexual purity is that big of a deal.

It may take a couple of dates before you're aware of what your date's values really are, but you can do a few things:

• Ask a friend what they KNOW (not just what they've heard) about the guy's/girl's morals.

• On the first or second date, ask him/her straight out: "These are my standards in dating, what are yours?" That puts things on the table right away and, hopefully, will take the pressure off both of you.

Brady, a Colorado Springs high school freshman, doesn't wait till the first or second date to ask. *Before* he actually takes a girl out on a date (both realizing they're already friends and want to go out with each other), he shares his dating standards with her. Then, if she can respect his guidelines, he meets with her parents and says the same thing to them.

What are his standards? "I want to become friends with your parents," Brady says, "and I want *you* to get to know *my* folks, too. So let's plan on doing things in each other's homes a lot—dinner, watching videos, playing games, listening to music."

"We're never going to be alone," he says. "I don't want to place you *or* myself in a tempting situation. I'm not ready for single-dating yet, so I want us to find group things to do with our friends.

"My relationship with God is very important to me; therefore, my church is also a high priority. I'd like you to be actively involved in the things my youth group does.

"And if I kiss you good night, it will always be with both of us standing up. I don't want us to get comfortable, sitting for long periods while kissing, so let's not even start. And we'll *never* lie down together—even when watching videos or TV. Let's just not place ourselves in that situation."

No, Brady is not a geek who can't get any dates. He's a normal guy with solid, immovable standards. A rarity, but a real good example.

Values include more than *physical* standards. They also include your priorities. Choose to date someone who places similar importance on things *you* think are important. For me (Susie), paying bills on time and being able to manage money is an important value.

Susie: I teach a young-adult Sunday School class, and one morning Bill showed up in my class. Because he was new, I introduced myself to him and we struck up a friendly conversation. A few weeks later he invited me out to dinner. Although I didn't know him very well, I thought he seemed like a nice guy and reasoned that dinner would give us a chance to get to know each other better. So I accepted.

It took me about 10 minutes to realize I did *not* want to have a dating relationship with this guy. See if you can grab the clue.

"Nice car, Bill. What year is it?"

"Ninety-four."

"Really nice. I like it."

"I don't know how much longer I'll have it."

"Oh, are you thinking about selling?"

"No, I really like it. But I keep forgetting to make my car payments, and it's in danger of being repossessed."

"You *forgot* to make your car payments?"

"Well, yeah. But only a couple of times. I'm in between jobs right now."

"Well, what kind of work are you looking for?"

"Something that doesn't require me to be on my feet."

"Hmmm. That puts a limit on it, doesn't it, Bill?"

"I'm not really worried about it. My parents are sending me money every month until I find something I like."

Knowing that I value managing money and paying bills on time, can you understand why I never went out with Bill again? Here's an adult who is allowing his parents to foot his finances while he takes me out to an exquisite Italian restaurant. Something is wrong with this picture.

What are the things *you* value? *Now* is the time to determine what's important to you. Then establish your dating relationships around your value system.

Looks

Let's be honest, guys. (It's me—Greg. We can afford to be honest with each other, right?) We're attracted to girls with a pretty face and a nice figure. And, girls, a young man with a well-built physique can certainly turn your head, can't he? Unfortunately, outward appearance is the ONLY standard many teens use in deciding whom to date. It's unfortunate, because often the best personalities aren't packaged in an absolutely drop-dead gorgeous body. (Actually, *most* aren't.) Many girls are plain or have minor "imperfections." And most guys sweat too much, don't always have smooth complexions and sometimes forget that their breath stinks.

There's nothing wrong with asking out a pretty girl, but there's equally nothing wrong with asking out a plain girl. (And, girls, same goes for you: Nothing is wrong in going out with the campus studmuffin, but there's equally nothing wrong with getting to know Mr. Very Average.) It all depends on what your goal is.

TIMEOUT!

WHAT'S YOUR GOAL FOR DATING?

You like the opposite sex—good. But are you wanting to date just so you can move up the popularity scale? Does dating a pretty girl give you a higher rating with the guys? Does going out with a popular guy rank you higher among the girls? Are you dating a girl because you hear she puts out? Or are your motives a little purer?

Although you're probably not thinking about choosing a lifetime mate, hanging around the opposite sex or dating can actually help with that eventual decision. By spending time with several types of people, asking questions and learning to become a good conversationalist, you're learning what kind of person will fit your unique personality. Discovering this stuff by doing fun things together is an added bonus.

Date to have fun, date to develop your relational skills with the opposite sex and date to see with what type of person you might want to spend your life.

INTERESTS

Should you date a volleyball player if you don't know a thing about the game? Do you date a math whiz if you flunked sixth-grade arithmetic? Maybe. And if you do, you'll feel most comfortable doing something in which you're both interested.

A good way to know if you're ready for dating is to see if you have anything in common with a guy/girl besides a physical attraction. A fast heartbeat is a poor reason to date. The reason? There will always be prettier girls or better-looking guys who will make your heart move a little quicker.

Have you ever wondered why more people don't date in junior high? Well, besides the obvious problems of immaturity, lack of wheels and not having a clue what to talk about, most guys and girls are still interested in things that only guys or girls would like to do.

Guys, remember how you hated to play with girls in grade school? The reason was that they didn't put together models or play army or football or transformers or baseball. You had nothing in common!

And, girls, remember how you thought every guy had "cooties"? You thought this because they didn't like to "play house," dress up your dolls or weave potholders to sell for a quarter. Again, you had nothing in common. This is true, too, in your early teen years. But as you mature, you develop more you can both relate to: studies, high school sports, choosing a college, bowling, videos, pizza!

Guys, I mention this to say that if everything you like to do is still "boy stuff," forget about girls for a while. Don't torture yourself by thinking you're weird because you're not interested in spending time with a girl. You're OK! Just wait till you're ready!

WATCH FOR A GODLY LIFESTYLE

If Jesus is number one in your life, chances are you won't be satisfied dating someone who doesn't "walk their talk." Though it may take a few dates to realize where a person's heart is at, be careful about forming a dating *relationship* with someone who *says* one thing inside church but *acts* another way outside of church.

I (Susie) once went out with a guy on a blind date. Maybe you've heard as many horror stories as I have about blind dates, but this guy was really neat. We had a great time together, and we had a lot in common. We were both in youth ministry, both enjoyed kids and both liked the same kinds of music. I really had a good time with him. As we continued to go out, though, I got to know him on a deeper level and realized this was not the guy for me.

Though he was a youth minister, he believed that what he did while away from the kids was his own business. I believe we ought to practice what we preach. He didn't tithe, and he had run up so many debts that he was in trouble with a finance company. (Why do I keep getting stuck with guys who don't have a clue about money?)

How could I establish a dating relationship with someone whose lifestyle wasn't a clear reflection of what Christ wants? I couldn't. We broke up.

Think about *your* dates. If you really want to establish a *committed* Christian dating relationship, then date godly people. Don't settle for less.

FOR FURTHER THOUGHT...

• What are some interests you hope you and your date have in common?

• What do you think about Brady's dating standards? Too loose? Too strict? Girls, how would you feel if the guy you wanted to date shared these standards with you and your parents? Guys, what standards would you share with your date and her parents?

• Susie mentioned the value of handling personal finances. What are some specific values you want your date to have?

• Why are we so hung up with looks when it comes to the opposite sex? If God looks at the heart, shouldn't we? How can we do that?

• Can you think of other good goals for dating?

• What can God teach you through dating?

????

DOLT or VOLT: Can You Carry On a Conversation?

Unless you go straight to a movie and then immediately home, you're going to have to make conversation, right? Though it's sometimes frightening, making conversation is one of the most important skills you can learn. Contrary to what you may have heard, you'll find that, for the rest of your life, most of your time with the opposite sex will be spent talking—even if you're a newlywed! You have a choice: You can be a DOLT or a VOLT.

A DOLT waits to be asked questions. When asked a question, he or she answers with one or two words and acts nervous, maybe even starts to shake a little. Granted, some DOLTS have parents who haven't taught them well. The family doesn't communicate, so springing into conversation doesn't come naturally. If that's where you are at, admit it. Then start practicing being a VOLT.

A VOLT is someone who not only *acts* interested in the other person, but he or she also IS interested. VOLTS are constantly thinking of new things to ask in order to get to know the other person better. If the other person is giving yes and no answers (a DOLT), the VOLT will change tactics and start asking questions that require a date to give longer answers. VOLTS are not afraid of silence; they just want to make the best use of their time.

CONVERSATION STARTERS FOR VOLT WANNABES

If you're already a VOLT, you know what it takes and what to ask to keep the conversation going. If you're not a VOLT—but would like to be one—here are a number of questions to ask:

Hey Greg:
    I have a buddy who dates a lot. Me? I can't even work up the nerve to call a girl on the phone. I guess I'm sort of jealous. Don't suggest I just learn to accept it; I've tried that. I need some ideas on how to quit being so jealous—and nervous. —Branson, Mo.

    GREG: You're jealous because you're comparing yourself with the wrong model. Cut it out! Looking to others as your guide is an awful habit to get into. Why? Because someone will ALWAYS be better than you in everything you do or try. The only one with whom you need to compare yourself is *you*.
    That's not saying you're the measure of everything; it *is* saying, "Base your feelings about yourself on the personality, the talents and the gifts God has given you—not what He's given others." If that means you need to accept yourself, I'm sorry. It's the right answer.
    One reason you're nervous is you're probably afraid of rejection—or "failure." Being scared is natural. In

fact, it's healthy. Certain things we *need* to fear. Fear motivates us to consider and reconsider what we're doing. Relating to the opposite sex is one of those things that needs constant reconsideration. Without it, we'll say or do something that could damage another person.

If you're confident around girls, you'll hopefully be doing the right things to make them feel comfortable and safe. If you learn what it takes to make a girl feel secure—and learn how to carry on a conversation—girls will call *you* for dates! *(But they'd better check with their parents first before they start calling guys, or they could get into major trouble! —Susie)*

STUFF GUYS DON'T MIND BEING ASKED BY GIRLS

• What kind of car would you like to have? Why?
• What do you think you'll study when you go to college?
• What bugs you about: home, chores, family rules, other guys your age, homework, teachers, walking the halls, lunchtime? *(Remember to ask WHY! If you don't ask it, most guys won't offer it.)*
• What kind of things have you collected through the years? How much is your collection worth? Why did you stop? What was so fun about it?
• What are your favorite sports to play? Favorite sports to watch?
• Do you believe in French kissing *before* the first date? *(If he says yes to this one, excuse yourself and call your parents to come pick you up!)*
• Are you good at video games? Which ones? Do you ever wonder why girls aren't as interested in video games as guys are?
• Who are your heroes? Is there anyone you'd like to be like?
• Have you ever read an entire book? *(Don't laugh. This is truer than you may realize.)*
• What's your dad like? Do you spend much time

together? What does he do for a living? Does he like it?

• Do you like the beach or the mountains? Why?

• When you go into a mall, what stores do you always visit?

• Have you thought about what songs you want sung at your wedding? (*This was a joke. Don't ever ask this question!*)

Dear Susie:

I've liked this certain guy for four years. He's real popular—a lot more popular than I am. I wrote him a note saying I'd like to do something sometime. He hasn't responded. I like him a *lot*. What should I do? —Boston, Mass.

Susie: There's nothing more you *can* do except continue to smile and be friendly. You've made it known that you're interested in getting to know him better. If he doesn't respond, it's obvious he doesn't care about establishing a friendship.

That hurts, doesn't it? But try to remember there will be guys *you're* not interested in who want you to like *them*. Don't forget what this hurt feels like. It will help you respond in kindness when the situation is reversed.

STUFF GIRLS DON'T MIND BEING ASKED BY GUYS

• If you could travel to any time period in history, where would you go and during which era?

• What's your favorite kind of perfume?

• Do you think guys should always call the girl, or should it work both ways?

• Do your parents let you call guys?

• What do you love most about your church?

• What's your favorite mall? Why?

• What types of movies make you cry?

• What do you think about people who cheat? Do you

think it's wrong? Why do you think they do it? Do you think the teacher knows?

- How do you feel about drinking?
- What movie have you seen that made you laugh hysterically?
- What's your favorite holiday? Why?
- What season of the year do you like most? Why?

- If you could create your own all-expenses-paid dream vacation, where would you go and what would you do?
- Any special traditions your family incorporates every Christmas?
- What do you think a kiss should mean?
- What do you think holding hands should mean?
- Do you think it's right to kiss on the first date?
- How are you like your mom? your dad?
- Do you have any pets?

STUFF YOU CAN BRING UP WITH EITHER

- Tell me about all of the different places you've lived.
- Who was your favorite grade-school teacher and why?
- What subjects have you always been good at? How about the not-so-good ones?
- What are the top-three memories you have of your grandparents?
- What are the top-three memories of experiences you've had with your dad? with your mom?
- Why do you think people drink or take drugs?
- How many of your friends come from divorced families? What do you think is the worst part about being from a divorced family?
- Have you ever had someone you know die? How did it happen? What do you think about death? (*You might want to wait until the third or fourth date for this one. But it's really a pretty good one when the conversation starts to lag.*)

• What do you picture heaven to be like? How about hell?

• How do you feel about people who really TRY to be popular? Why do you think they do that?

• When you watch the news or read the paper, what "gets" to you the most?

• How did (and do) your parents discipline you? Why would you get into trouble?

• What were your favorite toys when you were a kid?

• What are your favorite board games? card games?

• What movies could you watch over and over again? *(If the guy starts talking about slasher movies, it's time to remember that homework assignment due in an hour.)*

• What are some good books you've read?

• What magazines do you like to look through? (Brio *and* Breakaway *readers are definitely of higher intelligence and spirituality!)*

• Are you a morning person or a night person?

Some of these questions are just fun things to ask to keep from having dead air. Others will tell you something—perhaps something you need to know if you're going to date this person again: what their beliefs are, what their hobbies are, how they relate to their family, what their attitude is toward school, what their entertainment habits are.

Being friends with this person, and especially forming a longer-term relationship, will be 100 percent dependent on whether you can talk about things you have in common. These questions should give you the answers you need to make up your mind.

Dear Susie:

The more I cling to my boyfriend, the more he withdraws. What's the prob? —Chicago, Ill.

Susie: Guys don't want to date someone who is possessive. They want their space. It sounds as though your boyfriend is feeling trapped by you. Back off, or you'll lose him.

When we become possessive with our relationships, closeness dwindles. When we let go, however, and give people the space they need and the freedom they want, the relationship often blooms.

FOR FURTHER THOUGHT...

- Can you think of any other questions to ask the opposite sex during a date?
- Why is learning the art of conversation so important?
- What about the art of conversation is hardest for you? Listening? Trying to say exactly what you mean? Knowing what to say next? Not interrupting? What will you do to overcome that hurdle or practice so that it gets easier? With whom will you practice?

????

Modesty—Does Anyone HAVE It Anymore?

Let's play a quick word-association game. I'll call out a word, and you say the first thing that comes to your mind, OK?

Summer
Chocolate
Adventure
Vacation
Modesty

Of course, you already knew by the title of this chapter that the only word on this list I'm really interested in is "modesty." What kind of image does it bring to your mind? An older woman wearing a long, old-fashioned black dress? Someone with a high-collared, buttoned-up-to-the-very-top-button shirt?

Actually, modesty is a lot more than just clothing. It also includes actions, motives and integrity. But let's just stick to appearance for now.

YOU ARE WHAT YOU WEAR

Ever heard the saying, "You are what you eat?" I guess it's really true. Nutritionists tell us that whatever we put *into* our bodies eventually *makes* our bodies. So if you ate nothing but chocolate, in a few years you'd probably weigh 300 pounds. No muscle. No tone to your body. Just flab.

Likewise, you are also a reflection of what you wear; or vice versa, what you wear is also a reflection of you. Guys who wear supertight jeans and short speedo-type shorts send one message to girls who see them:

He's sure trying to flaunt himself, isn't he?

Unbuttoned shirts and a refusal to wear anything but tank tops or T-shirts with cut-off sleeves sends the same message:

He must really think he's impressing us with those muscles and those two chest hairs.

(Really. That's exactly what girls think.)

And girls who wear tight sweaters, tight skirts and short shorts also send a loud message:

She wouldn't be advertising if she didn't want someone to check out the merchandise. I think I'll ask her out.

And when she DOES go out with Handsy Hank, she can't figure out why he's coming on so strong. WAKE UP, GIRLS!

Loose dress reveals a loose heart. Whatever is on the inside will eventually come out. In other words, what we think about and feel strongly about will sooner or later show up in our lifestyle. Girls, if you're constantly thinking about how to turn on a guy, you'll eventually start dressing in a way that will turn him on. And guys, if you're constantly thinking about showing off parts of your body to a girl, you'll eventually try to do just that.

NOT A PROBLEM UNLESS...

It doesn't matter how you dress—unless you want to live a godly life. (And we hope that's your goal.) If you really want good dating relationships, then strive not to dress in such a way that will tempt your date. If you're both Christians, why would you want to make it tough for him/her to maintain sexual standards? Be an *enhancer* (one who complements your date's value system) instead of a *tempter* (one who could cause the other to relax his/her standards).

Dear Susie:

I'm prettier than my friend, but when I start liking a guy he always ends up liking *her!* What can I do? — Omaha, Nebr.

Susie: Your letter proves an age-old truth: Looks aren't everything! Personality is a big plus. Accessibility is another.

Think about the people you enjoy being around. Why do you enjoy their company? Probably because they make you feel good about yourself. They're secure. They're fun. They know how to laugh. They're not always worried about making a perfect impression. They're relaxed and comfortable. This, in turn, makes *you* relaxed and comfortable.

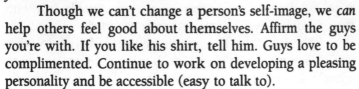

Though we can't change a person's self-image, we *can* help others feel good about themselves. Affirm the guys you're with. If you like his shirt, tell him. Guys love to be complimented. Continue to work on developing a pleasing personality and be accessible (easy to talk to).

IT ALL BEGINS WITH...

When you're getting ready for a date, think ahead of time about what you'll wear. God not only wants to live in our hearts, but He also wants to influence our thinking.

Do you mean He wants to make us puppets?

No, but God wants us to think thoughts that are reflective of Him. Check *this* out: "Fix your thoughts on what is true and good and right. Think about things that are pure and lovely, and dwell on the fine, good things in others" (Phil. 4:8, *TLB*).

So girls, when you're getting ready for a date and find yourself thinking, *I wonder how Jason would like this slip?* you're allowing your thoughts to go in the opposite direction of what God wants. Pull your thoughts back in and ask God's help in directing your mind to purer things. Likewise, when you're getting ready for bed and wondering if your boyfriend would find your nightgown sexy or not—STOP! and pray about your thoughts. In our dating years, God wants us to seek *modesty*—for our sake and for the sake of our dates.

WHAT GOD SAYS...

The Bible is extremely clear on modesty. "And the women should be...quiet and sensible in manner and clothing. Christian women should be noticed for being kind and good, not for the way they fix their hair or because of their jewels or fancy clothes" (1 Tim. 2:9,10, *TLB*).

In other words, God is telling us to use good judgment. Does He want to be a fashion killjoy? No way. I believe He has nothing against wearing what's *in* as long as it's in good taste and doesn't cause someone else to stumble (sin with their thoughts, eyes or actions) or be tempted.

Ephesians 5:1 tells us to be imitators of God. In other words, our goal is to *reflect* Him. If we're calling attention to ourselves, we're taking attention away from our heavenly Father.

If your perfume or cologne arrives at your church 10 minutes before you do, what does that tell you? Why wear so much? For Jesus? Strive to seek God's attention instead of man's.

WHAT KIND OF FACE ARE YOU PAINTING?

Too often, Christian girls walk into church looking as if the

Maybelline counter exploded on their faces. What? Do you think guys are attracted to that? (*We're not!* —*Greg*)

Most guys like girls who look natural. That means learning how to wear makeup to *enhance* your natural beauty instead of using it to become something you're not—like a fake painting.

THE CHALLENGE

According to Hollywood, we're supposed to be sexy, beautiful and alluring in order to be loved and accepted by others. We're bombarded with this false message by magazines, advertisements, movies and TV shows. Yeah, yeah, yeah. We *all* wanna be loved and accepted. But when we give our lives COMPLETELY to Christ, our need to imitate the world in order to be accepted changes. Our sights and goals are now fixed on something and Someone much more important— following Jesus and becoming like Him.

So here's the challenge. Time yourself for one week on how long it takes you to get ready every day (shower, hair, makeup—*everything*). Then commit that same amount of time to Jesus *daily* in prayer and reading your Bible.

For Further Thought...

- Guys, what turns you off about a girl's appearance?
- Girls, what turns you off about a guy's appearance?
- What does modesty mean?
- How can the way you dress be a positive or negative reflection of this Scripture?
- Is it possible to dress modestly and still look attractive and stylish? How?
- What points in this chapter did you agree with? disagree with?

????

DATING STUFF:
GUYS ONLY

Be a Hero!

YOU CAN HELP GIRLS BUILD
SENSATIONAL SELF-ESTEEM

What can be so fragile that it shatters with a disapproving glance? What can be so low a flea can't even do the limbo under it? What can be so easily influenced by every single thing a guy says or does?

What? No clues? Well, that's the problem, pal! It's a girl's self-esteem.

The way girls feel about themselves these days is under vicious attack. Flawless women on magazine covers and in makeup advertisements and megamodels are constant reminders that she doesn't measure up. If a girl lacks beauty, brains and bucks, society makes her feel as though she doesn't deserve to live.

That's where you come in. (You had the feeling I wanted something from you, didn't ya?) Each day, you have the choice to build up or tear down a girl's self-esteem with the things you say and do.

What am I getting at? Do I really mean it's high time to cut out the smart remarks and the ingenious nicknames? You got it. Here's your chance to follow seven simple steps that will make you a hero and a friend to the girls in your life.

1. Accept Her Physical Uniqueness

In other words, never talk about her body. How would you feel if you were constantly compared to a beefed-up Sly Stallone or pretty-boy Tom Cruise? Hey, it's even worse for a girl.

Sizing her up next to skinny or busty super-models, joking about her body parts or giving her a nickname based on a physical feature is an absolute, guaranteed esteem exterminator.

How can a girl accept her uniqueness with joy when guys are teasing her about her looks? She may not be a babe—yet. But telling a girl she's fat or ugly stabs her heart. It also insults God! (Check out Psalm 139:13,14.) He knit us together. That means He planned our appearance. We're each one-of-a-kind, original handiworks of God Himself.

So give her a break. Just as you'll grow into your feet, she'll come into a beauty all her own as she develops through these awkward years.

2. Overlook Obvious Oddities

Trust me, she already knows that today her hair resembles a troll doll. And even if there *is* dried mustard on her right cheek or lettuce hanging off her braces when she flashes you her pearly whites, control yourself! Hold off on the ol' point-and-stare stuff. Let her girlfriend in the next class-period break the news. She'll die if *you* tell her.

3. Treat Her Like a Lady

She may be stunned if you open the door for her or carry her lunch tray, but believe me, a girl wants to be treated like a lady.

When you punch her in the arm, call her a boy, pass gas in her presence or make her do everything for herself, a girl feels far from feminine. And for the guys who think a girl's rear is fair game—forget it! A holy hug is one thing, but tush-touching is totally off-limits! She'll feel cheap instead of cherished.

My point is this: You can make a girl feel like an angel or like ashes depending on the way you treat her. Check out 1 Thessalonians 5:11: "Therefore encourage one another and build each other up, just as in fact you are doing."

Oh yeah, one other thing: next time you're with a girl and you have to belch—swallow it!

Hey Greg:
I have a couple of friends who seem to go through a girl every other week. That is, they date them, get what they want, then dump them. I like these guys, but I think they're jerks with girls. What's wrong with these guys anyway? —Dearborn, Mich.

GREG: Guys learn how to treat girls from a lot of sources:

- Their dads (this could be good or bad)
- Older brothers (again, good or bad)
- Friends
- Movies, TV, HBO, MTV, music videos
- *Playboy* and other X-rated garbage

To be honest, what a lot of guys are choosing to follow—like your friends—isn't real-world stuff. That is, girls aren't ready and willing to do whatever it takes to please a guy. They're put together totally different. Sadly, a few girls feel they need to do whatever it takes to get and keep a guy, so some accommodate them; but it won't last long.

It sounds as though your friends have believed some bad information. You can try to convince them otherwise, but that kind of guy will likely say that *you* got some bad info! As much as we'd like to, it's tough to change other people. If these friends don't start doing things differently, they're never going to know the fun and wonder of having a lifetime relationship.

Respect is the ultimate key. Trust me; the kind of girls you want to spend time with want guys to respect them in every way. It's sort of a lost art, but I hope you're the kind who doesn't mind going against the tide.

4. COME TO HER RESCUE

"Get serious," you say.

I am.

"Wait. You mean I'm supposed to defend her in front of the guys? But they'll think I have the hots for her. She'll probably think I LIKE her."

OK, a quick lesson in priorities. A person's feelings are much more important than *your* reputation. How do I know? Because Jesus (our role model) proved it over and over when He cared for people's needs, unafraid of what others might think. (Read it yourself in Luke 13:10-17.)

Besides, you can *really* be a hero with this one. You can stamp out rumors, grab gossip by the throat, even rescue her on the spot when she's being verbally battered by other guys.

And hey, she'll tell all her friends what a nice guy you are. (*Shhh. Secret scoop:* Girls want to spend time with nice guys, not hormone hustlers!)

Girls like nice guys, not hormone hustlers.

5. BE HONEST ABOUT YOURSELF

Have you ever known people who seem so perfect not even their breath is bad? Next to them, you look like a mess, a wreck, a bundle of nerves.

But these people *do* have a problem; it's called being real. They think admitting struggles is a sign of weakness. That's pretty twisted thinking, isn't it? Being honest about yourself to others shows strength. It makes others feel as though you'll be able to understand when they have a problem.

So what's the point? Girls feel encouraged—sort of like they're not alone—when you open up. You don't have to spill your guts to every gal, but next time she's sharing about a family blowup, tell her about last week's big one with your dad. Along with feeling encouraged, she'll sense that you trust her. That's a foundation for a good friendship. True friends know all about us—and like us anyway! So open up. It'll be worth it.

6. RESPECT HER OPINIONS

Some guys feel cool and in control when they blast a girl's ideas. Yet they're communicating total disrespect for her.

When a girl trusts you enough to share her opinions, responding with an insensitive "that's a stupid way to feel" will either tick her off or send her into a shell. Insulting her and then laughing—that's a double tick-off! Not only do you run the risk of making her mad, but you'll also instantly lose her trust. And that may take months to regain.

Respecting her opinions helps a girl feel important. What a great way to boost her self-esteem! Plus, showing respect to others means you're catching on to the maturity thing.

7. REMEMBER, HER SOCIAL LIFE IS SACRED

Sadly, a lot of girls are BIG into believing that "boyfriend-lessness" is a fatal disease.

Dateless proms, Friday nights home with the family, being used and abused—all these are huge disasters to the average teen girl. She won't have those hyped-up romantic stories to share with her friends first thing Monday morning at school. Girls without guys feel as though they have REJECT stamped on their foreheads.

One youth-group night, I overheard Tom asking Michelle why she wasn't going out with anyone. As the blood drained from her face, you could almost hear her eyeballs and heart plop onto the pavement. I held my breath, waiting for her response. She was speechless. A shoulder shrug was all she could muster up. Obviously, Michelle wasn't going to smile and remark in a chipper tone, "Well, no one likes me, that's why." Yet that's how Tom's question made her feel.

So there you have it. Seven simple steps that will help girls feel sensational about themselves. Pack up your put-downs and encourage girls to be their best. Go ahead, be a HERO!

This article by Andrea Stephens first appeared in the February 1994 issue of *Breakaway*.

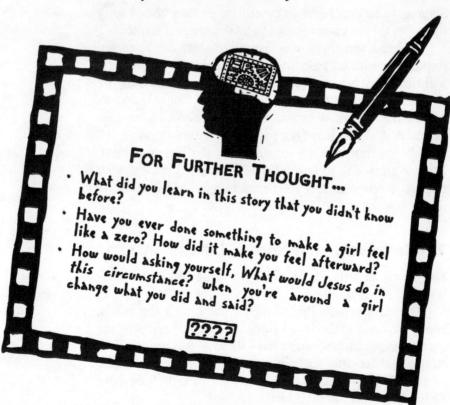

FOR FURTHER THOUGHT...

- What did you learn in this story that you didn't know before?
- Have you ever done something to make a girl feel like a zero? How did it make you feel afterward?
- How would asking yourself, What would Jesus do in this circumstance? when you're around a girl change what you did and said?

????

When Your Parents Don't Like Your Boy/Girlfriend

You've been dating Jeremy for almost a whole month. (If you're a guy, you can scratch out Jeremy and write in the name of any girl you think is cute. Because I [Susie] am writing this chapter, I'm going to use guys' names instead of girls'. So if you're a guy, just use your imagination and make it work, OK?) Suddenly, during dinner one evening, your parents say, "Honey, we don't think Jeremy's a good influence on you. We want you to stop seeing him."

You...

a. spit the remains of your half-chewed pork chop at your little brother who is giving you that "nyah-nyah-nyah-nyah-nyah" look.

b. sit in absolute shock for three whole hours, unable to

move (except for blinking, swallowing and breathing).

c. sarcastically remark that jungle life would be better than this and then announce that you're moving to Uganda.

d. pretend that you've suddenly gone deaf, calmly continue eating and then politely say, "May I be excused now? Jeremy and I are planning our elopement this evening."

e. ask if you can talk it out.

f. scream, yell, knock the table over, break all the dishes (except the Tupperware ones that *never* break) and, for added effect, throw your milk on your little sister.

g. cry hysterically; *so* hysterically that you start to hyperventilate.

h. call 9-1-1 and warn them of what's *about* to happen.

i. respond, "I really care for Jeremy. I don't understand why you're doing this, but you're my parents, so I guess I have no choice but to obey."

j. say, "Fine. Just fine. And I guess you won't be watching the news anymore?" (Makes no sense, but you're way past the point of making sense, and this is just the first thing that popped into your head that you could deliver dramatically.)

k. hold your breath until your face turns blue, hoping your mom will freak and say, "Oh, honey, we're so sorry. Your dad isn't being cohesive. Must be all that Pepsi he's been drinking." (You're thinking, *What does Pepsi have to do with anything? And is "cohesive" really the right word to use here? Doesn't that mean "to stick" to something? Or is that adhesive?* But hey, you're talking about the guy you think you might *love,* so you skip the vocabulary search and continue holding your breath until you lose consciousness. When you awake, you find yourself in a log cabin with a little black and white mutt running around, barking beside your bed. Someone calls him "Bandit," and he starts licking your hands. Your mom is placing a cold washcloth on your forehead while your dad leans over your bed, stroking your hair and calling

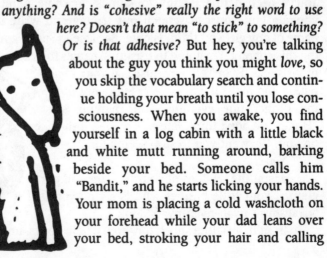

you "Half Pint." You have a strange urge to say, "I love you, Pa." But you refrain.)   Hmmm. Holding your breath is *never* a good idea, unless you're under water.

l. vow to become a nun or a monk—whichever has an immediate opening and pays the most.

m. scream, "You guys are sooo unfair! And so out of it! I just can't believe you!" Then you stomp down the hall to your bedroom and slam the door reallyreallyreally hard.

n. laugh hysterically.

o. continue laughing hysterically until they think you've lost it and make an appointment for you with a psychiatrist. But when they take you in for counseling, you suddenly become OK again and complain about how totally unfair your parents are.

p. spend the next three months in your bedroom because your parents grounded you for wasting their money on a counseling session in which all you did was complain about them.

q. dive into your schoolwork.

r. vow to write a book for teens about dating—one that will highlight all *your* expertise on the subject—so kids will no longer be deprived of your wisdom.

s. get out your old copy of *Getting Ready for the Guy/Girl Thing* to figure out where you went wrong.

t. scream, "Carol and Mike Brady would've *never* been so irrational with *their* kids!" Then act as though you're choking on a green bean just in case they weren't listening.

u. quote that verse from the Bible about parents not provoking their kids to anger—or something like that.

v. threaten to quit drinking water for the rest of your life.

w. throw yourself onto the floor, assume a fetal position, cry like a baby and scream, "I didn't ask to be born! I wanna go back!"

x. start quoting any Scripture verses you've memorized.

y. whisper, "OK, then. I'm just gonna bow down and worship idols."

z. say, "It's God's will that we be together."

Even though you know Jeremy a lot better than your folks do (after all, *you're* the one who is dating him, right?), the bottom line is that **God wants you to obey your parents** (see Eph. 6:1; Col. 3:20).

Even when they don't make sense?

Yeah, even then. The exception would be if your mom or dad tells you to break the law. Such as, "Honey, I'm running low on grocery money this week, so grab the shopping list and shoplift the groceries from the supermarket—wear my overcoat, OK?"

"But, Mom! That's against the law!"

"You heard me. Either do what I say, or your father and I won't let you date till you're 36."

This is the time *not* to obey your parents. But if your mom and dad are really asking you to *do* this, take the list and *act* as though you're going to obey them, but go directly to the police station instead.

Well, THEN what do I do?

Place the list on the receptionist's desk and say, "Look, I know I won't be able to date now till I'm 36, but I just can't steal."

You'll be heralded as a local hero and *everyone* in town will want to date you. But stay away from reallyreallyreally older girls and reallyreallyreally younger guys. (But hey, we'll cover that in another chapter, OK?)

Back to "What to Do When Your Parents Don't Like Your Boy/Girlfriend." **Answer:** *Obey them.*

You may think you have every right in the world to "set them straight," do your own thing, argue and scream till they're so sick of hearing you they give in—but guess what?

You really *don't* have that right.

If you're serious about God being numero uno (number one for those of you who are not bilingual), then *your* rights become *His* rights. In other words, He owns your rights.

To squeeze the fun outta your life? Nope. But because your heavenly Father has your best interests at heart, He has created a framework for us to live in. It works like this: (God's on top because He thought the whole thing up and because He's almighty and all-powerful.)

GOD

Mom and Dad

Children

So even if you don't *agree* with what your parents say, God still commands you to honor and obey them because they are in a position of authority over you. They will someday have to give an account to God about how they raised you, disciplined you and guided you through life. Pretty major responsibility, huh?

Sometimes they'll make mistakes. When they do, you don't have to jump up and down, screaming, "AHHHH! You really blew it, didncha?" Simply keep loving them, praying for them and obeying them.

Wanna know a secret? Your parents will see a TON of maturity in you (and trust you a bunch more) if you'll simply start obeying them

1 TON

without always screaming about it. And while you're obeying them and not liking it because you don't agree with their decision, be *praying* for them. If it's God's will that you and Jeremy be together, don't you think He's big enough to work it out? It's not *your* job to change the mind and heart of your mom and dad. Trust *God* to do it.

That's exactly what Emily did. Here's her story. (True—except I changed the names and cities.)

I grew up in Houston and went to a Christian college in Oklahoma City. That's where I met Dave my freshman year. He was from Miami, and we became good friends. Both of us were from conservative Christian families and both of our dads were in the ministry.

Dave was kind of wild his first year of college. Nothing really bad—just a lot of pranks that caused the administration to suspend him a few times. After our freshman year, we both went back to our hometowns and worked to save money for the following year.

During that summer, Dave really got serious about his walk with Christ. He also decided it was time to get serious about his studies, so he put the wild streak behind him. When I arrived back at college for my sophomore year, I saw a big change in his life.

He'd always been a popular guy, but now he was using his popularity to impact others for Christ. He became quite a leader on campus and led several students to a deeper relationship with God.

About halfway through our sophomore year, we started dating. I went home for spring break and told my parents all about him. I was sure they would share my excitement in dating such a wonderful young man. Instead, they took me by complete surprise.

"Honey, we've heard about Dave. We think he's too wild for you."

Well, I admit, his reputation from our first year at college had really spread. And since we were attending a denominational Christian college, news and newsletters traveled fast! It didn't surprise me that they knew about him.

"But you don't understand, Dad. Dave isn't like that anymore."

"Even so, Emily, your father's right. We don't want you associated with him."

"Mom, he's completely changed. He's such a spiritual leader on campus. And when we're together, we read the Bible, pray and talk about our goals. I've never dated anyone like him before. He knows where he's headed. He thinks deeply. He challenges me. I really like him." (She WANTED to say, "I LOVE him," but didn't think this was the right time.)

"Emily, we DON'T want you dating him anymore."

Well, I could have screamed. I could have brought up the fact that they were several hundred miles away from campus and, therefore, could not accurately judge what Dave was really like. After all, they'd never even met him.

I could have reminded them that I was in college now—an adult completely capable of making my own decisions. I was hurt. I was shocked. I felt like I would die.

And though I WANTED to scream, it seemed like God was saying, "It's OK, Emily. Obey them. Trust Me. Trust Me. Trust Me."

So, as a Christian, I did the only thing I felt I COULD do. I obeyed them.

"Mom, Dad. It kills me to hear you say these things. But you're my parents. I love you. Though it hurts like crazy, I'll obey you and not see Dave anymore. But will you do me a favor?"

"What's that, Em?"

"Promise me you'll pray about it. I want the man GOD has chosen for me. I feel like Dave might be him. But if he is, then God wouldn't ask me to go against your will. I do believe He'll show you if Dave's the man for me."

"Yes, Emily. We WILL pray."

I returned to campus after spring break and broke up with Dave. I hated doing it. I didn't know two people could cry so much.

"Em, I want to spend the rest of my life with you," Dave said. "But we need the blessing of your parents. That's part of

God's will. Let's both make ourselves date around, giving God a chance to change OUR hearts if we're not right for each other.

"But let's also continue to pray for OUR relationship and for God to change the hearts of your parents if we're to be together."

I went out with a few other guys, but none of them even came close to Dave. They all seemed surface. He dated other girls, but I knew he was still praying for our relationship.

That summer I spent three months in Nicaragua on a short-term missions trip. I went back to Houston just a week before school was to start.

"Mom, Dad. Are you still praying about Dave and me?"

"Yes, Em. We are. And we still feel it's best that you not date each other."

I could have died. I had been praying so hard and hoping so much that there would have been a change by now.

I went back for my junior year and kept my promise. I continued to obey my parents. Every now and then, Dave would see me across campus, wave, and run up to me and say, "Em, I'm still praying. Still believing. Keep obeying your mom and dad. We gotta believe God's big enough to do something if this is His will."

So I continued to pray. I also continued to date around. So did Dave. We both hated it. I went back to Houston for Christmas break. Even though it felt good to have over a month off from term papers and homework, I couldn't quit thinking about Dave. Would it ever work out? Should I try to forget him even though I wanted to spend the rest of my life with him?

God was number one in both of our lives. We had similar goals. He was preparing to be a doctor. I was heading for the nursing field. We both had a deep love for missions.

As I was packing and getting ready to return to campus at the end of our semester break, my parents came into my bedroom.

"Em, let's talk."

I shut the suitcase and sat on the edge of my bed.

"Emily," my dad began. "We've watched you closely the last couple of years. You don't seem to be as happy as you used to be."

"The spark is gone from your eyes," Mom interjected.

"And we've been praying about you and Dave," Dad continued. "You know how strongly we've felt. But honey, after all this time of praying, and from seeing your obedience to us when we know you've felt the opposite, we've been hearing God's voice in a new direction.

"We now have a peace about Dave, Em. God has told us to trust Him. He's overwhelmed us both with a deep, settled peace about you two."

My eyes flooded with tears. I grabbed my parents and hugged them tightly. They began to cry, too.

"Emily," Dad continued. "Thank you for obeying us. If you had gone behind our backs, we would have never had the deep peace we have now."

"That's right, honey," Mom said. "Thanks for being patient with us and trusting God to do the changing. Nothing's impossible for Him, is it?"

Well, you can imagine how excited I was to get back to campus. Dave and I knelt in the campus prayer chapel, crying and praying for hours.

"It pays to do it God's way, doesn't it, Em?" he said.

I choked back the tears and nodded my agreement.

Dave and Emily now have a fantastic Christian marriage and four beautiful kids. He's a successful doctor and often offers his medical services to the needy on various long- and short-term mission extravaganzas.

Emily knew the secret—God's ways are best. When it *seems* as though it doesn't make sense, TRUST HIM. If it's God's will for you and your boy/girlfriend to be together, He's certainly big enough to work it out.

Yeah, but what if my parents aren't Christians? And they're not willing to pray about it?

What do you think is going to be a bigger witness to them? Your screaming and demanding your own rights? Or reacting in obedience and praying that God will change their hearts?

They're going to see Jesus through your *actions*. So it doesn't matter if your mom and dad are Christians or not. God is still big enough to work it out. His will WILL be done!

Dear Susie:

This guy I like is really shy. I think he likes me, but is too shy to ask me to go steady. How can I encourage him so he'll have the nerve to ask me? —Filer, Idaho

Susie: You can't *force* him to ask you *anything*, but you *can* help him feel good about being around you. Always smile and be friendly to him. Guys like to be needed so ask him questions about the homework assignment (or something else you have in common). Bake a batch of cookies for him or compliment him on things he does well. This will show him you really care about him.

If, after all that, he *still* doesn't show any response, back off. He's obviously not interested and doesn't want to hurt your feelings. If you continue to plant yourself in his path, he'll think you're a pest.

Dear Susie:

I've been hurt, so I've stopped dating for a while. Now, I want to get back into the dating scene, but I'm scared of getting hurt again. Got any advice? —Fort Wayne, Ind.

Susie: Start slowly by choosing to group-date or double-date. You'll feel less threatened if you're around several people. As your confidence begins to build, concentrate on establishing some solid singular-guy friendships.

There's no way to avoid being hurt. Instead of focusing on the pain, try to understand that you serve a God who can make beautiful things happen out of devastating situations. Ask Him to comfort you and help you learn from the hurt. Then trust Him to guide you back into good relationships when the time is right.

FOR FURTHER THOUGHT...

- Describe a specific time in your life when you totally disagreed with your parents but realized later they were right.
- What's the toughest thing about being obedient to your folks?
- Do you and your parents pray together regularly? When was the last time? (If not, would you pray about approaching them to pray with you?)
- What "rights" are the hardest for you to submit to God?
- Are you able to obey your parents when it comes to your relationships?
- If so, what has God taught you through that?

????

PART III

Love Versus Lust
Being in Love with Love

Are You in Love with LOVE?

Mindy was a good student; she pulled mostly B's. She sat in the second row, third seat from the back in my junior English class. Though she had a lot of friends, she hadn't dated much. She sometimes had a hard time staying awake in class because of her paper route.

Every day of the week, Mindy rolled out of bed around 3:30 in the morning. While the rest of the world was still snoring and dreaming about chocolate-filled, sugarcoated donuts, she was rolling papers, loading them in her car and beginning her route.

She met Tony—a high school senior—through a mutual friend. After being friends for a couple of months, they began dating. A few weeks later, he lost his job. Mindy talked to her boss and helped Tony land an early-morning route.

Because their routes were near each other, they decided to work together. Each morning they met at 3:45, rolled papers, loaded them in his car and tossed the latest news to their section of America.

They usually finished about 5:15. As their relationship deepened, Tony started coming home with Mindy after the route and sleeping on the couch downstairs while she went back up to bed.

You can guess how long *this* lasted, can't you? A couple of weeks later, while the rest of the family was still asleep, Tony and Mindy were both in *her* bed, catching a few winks before her 6:30 alarm went off for school.

And you can guess how long *just sleeping together* lasted, can't you? A few weeks later, Mindy lost her virginity. It was just too easy, too convenient. *Besides*, she thought, *I love him! I wanna spend the rest of my life with Tony. And he loves me. Why NOT make love to each other?*

Though they attended separate high schools, they found a way to be together more. Both professed to be Christians, but Mindy was not from a Christian home; and her relationship with Christ resembled more of a roller-coaster ride than anything else. She began attending Tony's church.

Tony had been praying about becoming a youth minister for the past year. "I really want to do something for God," he had said. "And I think the Lord is calling me to youth work."

Mindy was excited about his call, even though it meant he'd be going away to a Christian college an hour from where they lived. He promised they'd keep in close touch her senior year and then she planned to join him on campus the following year.

Tony left for college and kept his promise. He came home several weekends that first semester, and Mindy visited him on campus. Their relationship continued to progress—physically.

By the end of that first semester of her senior year in high school, Mindy told me they were engaged. "We're getting married right after my graduation," she said.

I (Susie) begged her to wait at least another year. "Wouldn't you like the experience of living in the dorm, running down the hall for popcorn, making close college friends whom you'll keep the rest of your life?"

No way. She wanted to be married as soon as possible. "We're in love," she kept saying. "We're in love. We shouldn't have to wait."

"But it's going to be tough to pay college bills, apartment rent and all that stuff," I continued. "What would it hurt to wait one year—or even one semester—just to give you some experience of being single and out of high school?"

"No, we're in LOVE!" she emphasized.

Secretly, I wondered if she was *really* in love, or if she was just in love with love itself. Mindy was dying to get out of the house. She was from a dysfunctional environment, received absolutely *no* affirmation from her parents and constantly fought with both of them. Tony was obviously filling a void in her life. He made her feel special, loved and needed.

"Nothing's going to change," she assured me. "Tony's still going to prepare for youth ministry, and I'll be an art major."

Well, they *did* get married—immediately following high school graduation. And even though she *said* this wouldn't happen, Tony didn't go back to college. There were too many bills to pay. She took a few classes at a local college until she learned she was pregnant. After Daniel was born, neither one of them went back to college. Now there were *three* mouths to feed. They needed a bigger apartment. Tony was always tired—and that was understandable. He worked hard as a roofer. When he finally got home at night, he was too bushed to make *anyone* feel special. It was all he could do to take a shower and fall into bed, only to get up the next day and do it all over again.

A couple of years have passed, and Tony's still working hard at the same job. Mindy now wonders what happened to her dreams of becoming an artist. Their marriage? It's rocky. Tony met a girl who was just like Mindy *used* to be: She was fun, outgoing and made him laugh. You guessed it. They had an affair.

Because Tony and Mindy really *want* to do what's right, they're trying to put the pieces back together. Going to church is hard because they've been so inconsistent the past few years. They're seeking Christian counseling and *want* to make it work, but Tony still wrestles with the guilt of not fulfilling God's call to the ministry, and Mindy sometimes blames Tony for her unfulfilled art dreams.

Were they really in love? Or were they simply in love with love? Whether you're a teen or an adult, it's easy to fall in love with an *idea*. We want to assume the person who makes us feel needed, loved and special will fit snugly into our dreams and God will bless our union and then we'll live happily ever after. But just because we're in *love* doesn't necessarily mean we're in love with the person we're dating. Oftentimes—especially for those who haven't dated a lot—we find ourselves simply falling in love with love.

How can you know the difference? Here are a few key questions to think through that will help you find out:

AM I IN LOVE WITH LOVE?

1. Is it this specific PERSON I want to spend the rest of my life with, or do I simply want to be married really bad?

2. Am I thinking, *He/she will make me happy. This person is everything I've ever wanted?* (Wake up: Prince Charming and Cinderella only exist in fantasyland.)

3. Are there reasons I want to be with him/her other than simply being together? In other words, are you anxious to leave home? Are you wanting to get out from underneath parental authority?

4. Why is THIS the right person for me rather than someone else?

5. What do my parents, youth leaders or pastor think about how the relationship has progressed?

6. Am I able to pray about whether or not *God* wants me to be with this person? Or do I think I already KNOW what He wants?

Dear Susie:

A few days after my 15th birthday, I lost my virginity. I'd had several boyfriends before this, but I wouldn't do anything (but make out) unless I got something back—like love or some kind of commitment.

Mark (my boyfriend) didn't pressure me. It's just that when I'm with a guy I really like, I lose myself. I want to be loved and accepted so badly that I do anything. It hurt physically. And we didn't use protection, but I didn't get pregnant. From that time on, I vowed I would always insist on using a condom.

Some people found out that we had sex and since he's 19 and I'm only 15, he may risk going to jail.

I really feel bad about it. I know what I did was wrong in God's eyes, but I can't forgive myself because I know I'll do it again.

I'm active in my church and always give money in the offerings. And I know other people who do OTHER sins—like criticize others and talk about them behind their backs. So is THIS sin really so bad?

I just want to be loved and have a companion. —Austin, Texas

Susie: First, let's start with the sin: "Other people do OTHER sins—so is THIS one really so bad?"

I believe (based on God's Word) that all sin is equal. There's no such thing as a big, bigger or biggest sin. *BUT* (and here's the catch) the Bible tells us that *no other sin* affects us as sexual sin does.

Let's chat for a second about your need to be loved and accepted. Know what? You're normal!

We all want that. God created that desire within each of us. Nothing is wrong with *feeling* or *wanting* that; but how we go about FILLING that need *can* be dangerous, especially if we're going against God's will to do it. And, yes, sex before marriage is wrong—as you've stated.

I don't know what kind of home you're living in or anything about your past; but many times when a girl is abused, she looks for love and acceptance by being free with the guys.

Also, many girls who don't have a loving relationship with their fathers (or if their fathers don't show them a lot of affection) will seek it from the guys they date. The problem? Though they're *looking* for LOVE, what they're *getting* is sex. Two very different things.

I'm proud of you for being active in church, giving money in the offerings and having a tender conscience (knowing what you've done is wrong in God's eyes). But the bottom line is: God would much rather help you live a holy life than have you keeping tabs on how much of your allowance you've dropped in the offering plate.

"I know I'll do it again," you say. Hmmm. Maybe you feel you've started a pattern you can't break. And it *will* be tough. It's similar to walking up a very steep hill after you've been used to zooming downhill without brakes. But you *can* reverse your actions. You don't *have* to continue the pattern you've begun.

But you won't be able to turn things around in your own strength. This takes the POWER of the Holy Spirit—God living in and through you. How do you get that power? Total surrender. Admitting to Him that you can't overcome this on your own. Can you do that?

Would you also ask God to send you a trusted adult with whom you can share this? That adult friend can help hold you accountable—in a gentle, positive way—and help you become all God wants you to be.

If you *want* to change your dating behavior, I invite you to pray this prayer:

> Lord, I know what I did was wrong. Please believe me when I say "I'm really sorry." Will You forgive me? I don't want to go against Your will.
>
> Lord, I'm going to be very honest right now. Even though I seek Your forgiveness and even though I'm saying I want to change, there's a part of me—way deep inside—that wants to keep doing what I've started. So I'm asking You to help me go against the desires of my flesh. Give me the strength not to give in. I know I can't overcome this in my own power. So I surrender my entire life to You and ask You to flood me with YOUR power—Your Holy Spirit.
>
> I commit my entire life and actions—and dates—to You, Jesus. When I *want* to go farther physically than I should, help me *not* to rely on my own strength—I know I'll fail. Instead, remind me that I have a greater power to stand on—the power of Your Holy Spirit.
>
> Lord, thanks for forgiving me. Thanks for seeing me as a pure child—whole. Please send a spiritually solid adult into my life with whom I can talk about all this—someone who can help me establish godly dating relationships. Amen.

For Further Thought...

- Have you ever been in love with love? How can this be dangerous?

- How can you help a friend who is simply in love with love?

- Do you believe God can give you wisdom and discernment? Will you begin praying now and asking Him to give you wisdom and discernment in regard to your dating life? Read James 1:5.

- Are you willing to listen to what others say about your dating life, or do you tend to be hardheaded?

- When has God's Holy Spirit enabled you to do something you couldn't have done on your own?

????

Dating + Love = Marriage— Then Sex

We've been talking about dating. And in a few minutes we'll chat about sex. But that missing ingredient somewhere in the middle is called L-O-V-E! How do you get from dating to love? And how do you get from love to marriage?

Well, I think we need to be honest here for a few minutes. Ready? It's an extremely slim chance that the person you date in high school will be the person you'll eventually marry. Stick with me and I'll give you a couple of reasons why, OK?

DATING IS A PROCESS

Dating isn't the open-ended gate that leads to marriage; it's a *learning time*. Dating is sort of an adjustment period—a time when you learn to relate with the opposite sex. Carrying on a conversation may *seem* easy, but it's really an art and it takes skill and practice.

Instead of thinking of your date as your future mate, try to see your time with him/her as a terrific opportunity to learn some necessary things you'll *need* once you DO fall in love. This is the time to learn certain signals from the opposite sex—a time to understand them better.

For instance, guys, when a girl compliments you on what you're wearing, do you automatically assume she likes you? And girls, when a guy says "hi" to you in the hallway, do your thoughts go wild, thinking he's going to ask you out? Lack of good communication with the opposite sex is one of the biggest frustrations teens face. So let's straighten out a few twisted thoughts.

GIRLS, guys want you to know the following:

• Sometimes we just want to *talk* with a friend who is a girl. Why is it that when we call, you start thinking we *like* you?

• And when we pass you in the hall at school and don't say "hi" (even though we're friends), don't jump to conclusions and start thinking, *Oh, no! He doesn't like me anymore?* Why can't you *think* first? Perhaps the coach just chewed us out, or we bombed a pop quiz in history or we were up late the night before and didn't get much sleep.

Dear Susie:

How come if you like a guy and he doesn't like you, you're attracted to him? But once he starts to like you back, you don't feel the same way about him? —Wheatland, Wyo.

Susie: What you've described is what's known as "the thrill of the chase." Sometimes a girl will set her sights on a specific guy and "hunt him" until he becomes interested in her. You've already pointed out the problem. Once he's interested in her, the thrill of the chase is gone.

This is not an honest way of establishing good friendships *or* good dating relationships. I hope you won't continue to simply just pick someone to like and then go blindly after him.

When you're attracted to a guy, ask yourself *why* you're attracted to him. Looks? Popularity? Clothes? I hope it's much more than this, because those are all surface things.

I hope you're attracted to the deeper qualities of a guy that really make or break a relationship: his relationship with Christ, his values, his lifestyle.

• We're *not* going to ask you out if we're not 90 percent sure you'll accept. So if we *are* tossing out signals (hanging around ALL the time, calling you excessively and joking with you a lot), please return a few signals. If you don't, we'll assume you won't go out with us, and we won't take the risk of asking.

• Yeah, sometimes we misread your signals. Be patient with us. This communication thing can be tough.

GUYS, this is what girls want *you* to know:
• Pay attention to us when we're trying to get *your* attention. When we notice you and think you're cute, we'll probably approach you. But when we do, don't be so engrossed in talking about last night's football game that you tune us out. LOOK at us. It's really hard sometimes for us to get your attention!

• Sometimes we *think* you want to ask us out, but we're not sure. Could you be a little more obvious when giving signals? Here's the deal: We become good friends with you. Then, without even planning on it, we start *liking* you—yes, as more than a friend. But we're scared to do or say anything about it because we're afraid it'll wreck our friendship. It often seems like a no-win situation: We risk losing your friendship and aren't sure we're going to gain something better. Sometimes we think it would be best to stick with you as a buddy and never get to know you on a deeper level.

• As much as we scream, "Equal rights!" deep down inside we really enjoy being around guys who take the lead, show initiative and display confidence. Know what that does for *us*? WE feel better about ourselves when we're around you.

• Yeah, sometimes we misread your signals. Be patient with us. This communication thing can be tough.

WHEN HAVE YOU BEEN MISREAD BY A GIRL?

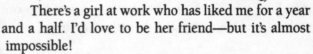

Six guys speak out!

Greg Baker, 17
Atlanta, Ga.

There's a girl at work who has liked me for a year and a half. I'd love to be her friend—but it's almost impossible!

It seems like the *slightest* bit of attention from me is blown completely out of proportion. I'm talking about *little* things—like just smiling at her and saying "hi."

Whenever I do that, she won't leave me alone. I mean, she starts hanging on me, putting her arms around me and stuff.

When I act apathetic, she accuses me of hating her. It's a no-win situation.

It's really kind of sad, because she's actually a pretty fun girl. But I have to hold back from being nice to her just so she won't get the wrong idea.

Justin Parsons, 17
Oklahoma City, Okla.

Recently, I took a girl out for a really fun evening just as friends. I started the date by giving her a rose, then took her to a cool Italian restaurant. Afterward, we went to a nearby park and fed the ducks.

I wasn't sure if I wanted a dating relationship, so

I didn't kiss her; we ended the evening with a hug.

Still, I sensed she had read too much into my actions and now wanted a full-scale relationship.

Matt Davis, 17
Portage, Ind.

There's a new girl at my school. She sits next to me in government class and obviously likes me. I'm nice to her and enjoy being her friend, but I don't go out of my way for her or treat her different from any other female friend.

Last weekend our school had a retreat that we both attended. She heard me telling some friends about a waterfall back in the woods and later asked me about it.

All I said was, "Some of us will probably hike there tomorrow if you want to come along."

Know what she did? Told the whole camp that she and I were going there together and no one else would be allowed to come.

Why do girls get the wrong idea when we guys try just to be friendly? I don't want a girl to fall at my feet. I like a challenge—after all, the pursuit is half the fun of dating!

Lance Britton, 17
Colorado Springs, Colo.

I enjoy talking with my friends, so from time to time I'll call a girl just to talk. More often than not, she thinks I'm *interested* in her when I really just want to be good friends.

Seth Toler, 15
Brentwood, Tenn.

Our youth group recently had a Friday night lock-in at my church. We had a great time but didn't get any sleep at all—that's the objective of an all-nighter, right?

I was busy on Saturday and didn't get completely caught up on sleep, so when I ran into a friend on Sunday I was still tired.

She tried to start a conversation with me, but I was too sleepy to concentrate on what she was saying. I could hardly keep my eyes open, let alone say anything intelligent!

Her reaction? She thought I didn't want to be her friend anymore.

I apologized to her later and we worked everything out, but I wish girls wouldn't jump to conclusions.

Denton Everett, 17
Bethany, Okla.

I've spent the past few weeks getting to know this girl by talking on the phone and going to her house. I've enjoyed becoming better friends with her, so yesterday I wrote her a note telling her that.

She immediately got defensive—as if I was asking for a commitment or something. I just wanted her to know that I liked her and looked forward to getting to know her better.

She reacted like I was trying to put a ring on her finger. She wrote me back saying we need more time to get to know each other. I'm thinking, *Isn't that what I said?*

Maybe it's just a lack of communication, but she's jumping ahead of me. I wish girls would slow down and not read more into what guys are saying.

✳

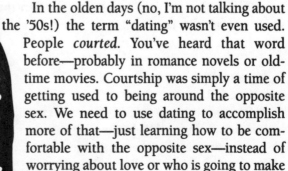

In the olden days (no, I'm not talking about the '50s!) the term "dating" wasn't even used. People *courted*. You've heard that word before—probably in romance novels or old-time movies. Courtship was simply a time of getting used to being around the opposite sex. We need to use dating to accomplish more of that—just learning how to be comfortable with the opposite sex—instead of worrying about love or who is going to make the first move.

YOU LEARN AS YOU GROW

The more you date, the clearer the picture you begin to develop of the kind of person with whom you want to spend the rest of your life. That's another reason why you probably won't marry the guy/girl you date in high school. The first few people you date will help you establish what you want and don't want in a lifetime partner.

Instead of dreaming up some perfect forever-mate, learn to be flexible. NO ONE is perfect. You'll never find the knight in shining armor or the princess. We *all* get broccoli stuck between our teeth, and we *all* get dirt underneath our fingernails.

So instead of dreaming about the perfect spouse, why not begin praying for God to help *you* become everything your future mate will need? Pray for the development of patience. Seek wisdom. Strive to live a life of integrity. Deepen your spiritual roots. Too many teens make the mistake of thinking, *When I fall in love with the person I want to marry, I'll become a better person.* NOW is the time to start becoming that better person!

AND THEN COMES LOVE

I think most of us have it backward. We seem to think that the person we fall in love with is the person we'll marry. Though love is an essential ingredient of marriage, the truth is, you may actually fall in and out of love *several* times before you finally find the person you'll marry.

How can that happen? Easy. Here is a scenario that illustrates it perfectly.

Jamie and Eric dated for a whole year. Jamie was head-over-heels in love with him, but Eric was just in deep-like. He worked the evening shift at Taco Bell and met a new employee who had just moved in from out of state. She and Eric hit it off quickly, and he decided he wanted to date around. Jamie and Eric broke up, and Jamie eventually began dating someone else—Alan.

Alan was crazy about Jamie, but she had just finished her senior year, and her plan was to head off to college. Alan still had one more year of high school left. *He* was *serious*; he even gave her a promise ring during spring break. But Jamie didn't want to be tied down when she got to school.

Once Jamie arrived at her small Christian college, she met Jeremy in freshman English. They started dating, and it didn't take Jamie long to fall hard. THIS guy was terrific! He was everything she wanted in a lifetime partner. But eight months into the relationship, Jeremy's ex-girlfriend transferred to the same college, and the old flame began to burn again. Jamie and Jeremy broke up, and eventually she began another relationship.

That's how it works for most people before they finally find the person they want to marry. Though *you* may not fall in love with several people, the fact is, you *could*. So the person you'll marry probably won't be the one you're in love with the first few times.

STEPPING STONES

You need to tiptoe on several important stepping stones before you make the step from love to marriage. Again, asking yourself some honest questions is the first place to start:

Is this the person GOD wants me to marry?
Although today you may not be able to imagine living without him/her, if it's not God's person for you, you'll only be miserable in the long run. So make each dating relationship a matter of prayer. And when you think you're falling in love, suggest that the two of you begin praying together (if you are not doing so already).

Will I have to make some compromises to marry this person?
Yes, we *all* have to give and take, but look a little deeper. Will you have to relinquish major

goals to spend the rest of your life with him/her? (And it can be OK to give up your dreams in exchange for other dreams. But make sure you really *want* to surrender those goals, or you'll hold it against your partner later in life.)

Some things should never be compromised. For instance, if the person you're in love with isn't a Christian and won't go to church with you after you're married, you'll be giving up the dream of having a husband/wife who is involved in the Lord's work with you. Even though you're in love *now*, it won't be worth it *later*. Surrender the relationship to God and trust Him to give you someone else—or allow Him to fulfill you in other ways.

Hey Greg:
There's a girl at school who I'm pretty sure likes me. In the hallway, she always walks by me real close. Sometimes she tries to touch me with her chest or hands. One time, she even put her hand on my rear while I was opening my locker! I haven't dated this girl, and it makes me uncomfortable just to see her. What's her problem? —Manassas, Va.

GREG: Wonder no more—you're being sexually harassed! Though it's more common for girls to complain that guys are grabbing body parts, it's happening to more and more guys.

The problem is, we have a sexually sick society, and tons of teens have the disease. Somewhere along the line—from friends, pornography (movies or magazines), perhaps even a parent or sibling—guys and gals are picking up the message that bothering someone in a sexual manner is what the other person *really* wants—that it turns them on. Or, they could simply be trying to get their "jollies" by seeing what they can get away with.

Unless there's a reversal in moral standards in the media (don't hold your breath) and the government, sexual harassment will continue. In the spring of 1993, the *New York Times* reported on a student survey of what types of behavior had happened to them. Here's what teens said:

- Sexual comments, jokes, looks (girls 76 percent, boys 56 percent)
- Touching, grabbing in a sexual way (girls 65 percent, boys 42 percent)
- Brushed against in a sexual way (girls 57 percent, boys 36 percent)
- Flashed or mooned (girls 49 percent, boys 41 percent)
- Target of sexual rumors (girls 42 percent, boys 34 percent)
- Had clothes pulled in a sexual way (girls 38 percent, boys 28 percent)
- Given unwanted pictures, notes (girls 31 percent, boys 34 percent)
- Blocked, cornered in a sexual way (girls 38 percent, boys 17 percent)
- Target of sexual messages, graffiti (girls 19 percent, boys 19 percent)
- Forced to kiss someone (girls 23 percent, boys 14 percent)

The study went on to say that much of this behavior first starts in sixth and seventh grade!

What can you do? If you want this girl's behavior to stop, you're going to have to do more than look disgusted and walk away. You're going to have to tell her. If you don't, she'll think you really like it and won't have any reason to stop.

P.S. If you or any of your friends are doing anything similar to girls, take the lead, be different; start respecting the opposite sex enough to keep your hands and words to yourself.

Does this person have my best interests at heart?

If he/she loves you because you enhance their career, their image or their self-esteem, you're not in love with the right person.

Bottom line: It's possible to fall in love with the wrong person! Again, you must get back to letting God control your dating relationships. He wants your happiness and fulfillment *even more than YOU do!*

Can you trust God to guide you in and out of your dating relationships? Will you place your faith in His direction, believing He's big enough to bring just the right person along at just the right time?

I (Susie) am in my 30s. And, as I mentioned before, I'm single and have never been married. Am I worried? Have I panicked? No. I've found real freedom in trusting my future to Jesus Christ. Do you know what that does? It takes all the pressure off *me!* Whenever I meet new guys, I don't have to think, *How can I get his attention? I wonder if he likes me? Will he ask me out?* I can relax in just being myself (friendly, fun, approachable) and trust God to work it out if it's His will for anything to happen.

But what am I going to do until He *does* bring the right man into my life? Sit around and think, *Why aren't I married?* No way! I'm having a total blast in life! I'm hopping on a plane about every other weekend, creating books and plays, teaching Sunday School, trekking through the jungle of Uganda, Africa—I'm fulfilled!

Can *you* find that same source of peace and security until God brings the right person into your life?

I LOVE HER. SHE LOVES ME. WE FEEL GOD GUIDING US INTO MARRIAGE.

When God *does* give the go-ahead for marriage, you'll know. Yeah, I know. Some of you are wondering if it's possible for you to miss God's mate for you.

I like to think of it as a big, exciting treasure hunt. Imagine this, OK? Imagine you have a five-year-old son. (We'll call him Ryan.) You get up early one Saturday and hide a ton of fun stuff in your big backyard. You've hidden some little cars under rocks, candy behind trees, a water gun underneath the swing, and waaay over by the sandbox—buried about six inches under the ground—you've hidden a bright, shiny treasure box filled with stuff you know he'll go CRAZY over.

You're jazzed. I mean, I cannot wait to wake him up and start him on this fun treasure hunt. Ryan runs outside and begins collecting the gifts you've placed in his backyard. You stand on the patio and watch, smiling and gloating in his success at finding the treasures.

An hour has passed and Ryan has found everything except the treasure chest. He knows there's one more big prize left, so he heads in the direction of the hedge to find it. It's nowhere near the hedge! You buried it next to the sandbox. Imagine how much you want your son to find that treasure. Would you stand quietly on the patio never saying a word?

NO! If you're like me, you're going to give him some pretty clear directions. "Hey, Ry! You're headed in the wrong direction. Come back this way." He starts toward the garage. Will you stand silently? I don't think so. You're so excited for him to find your gift, you're going to make it as obvious as you can. "No, Ryan. It's not over there. Head toward the sandbox, OK?"

It works the same way with God. He wants you to find His gifts even more than *you* do! As your loving Father, will He stand silently and simply watch you head in the wrong direction? No. He'll do everything He can to let you know where His treasure is waiting. That's why daily communication with the Lord is so important. The more time we spend with Him, the clearer His will for our lives becomes.

You'll probably fall in love with a few treasures before you actually find HIS treasure created specifically for you. Even though you may *think* nothing else could be more beautiful, trust Him with the valuables. *His* lifetime-treasure-mate will fulfill you far more than anyone you find on your own.

I'VE FOUND GOD'S TREASURE!

When God gives you an overwhelming sense of peace about the person you love and you're both heading toward marriage, it's time to seek wisdom and advice from your pastor. Many couples these days are receiving "preengagement" counseling. At minimum, you'll want to get some Christian premarital counseling before you actually exchange vows. Use the engagement process to hammer out details such as, finances (Who will balance the checkbook? Will you have separate or joint accounts? Will you use charge cards?); children (Do both want children? How many children does he/she want?); church preference (Will she go to his church, or will he go to her church? How important is church involvement to the both of you?); and other important matters through which your pastor can guide you.

Above all, keep Christ as the very CENTER of your relationships; and, yes, that includes dating, falling in love, breaking up, falling back in love, becoming engaged and eventually getting married.

FOR FURTHER THOUGHT...

- What's the most difficult thing for you to understand about the opposite sex?
- What are some "mixed signals" guys often give? What are some "mixed signals" girls often give?
- At this point in your life, how do you decide whether you're in love with someone?
- How can you know if the person you're dating is the one God wants you to marry?
- How can your prayers about this relationship help you decide whether you're truly in love (or just in love with love), know if the person you're dating is the one God wants you to marry and know if you are ready to get married?

????

Real Love or Real Lust?

"God is love" (1 John 4:16), and His Word gives us an in-depth description of how genuine love expresses itself. First Corinthians 13, often called "The Love Chapter," spells out the real meaning of love. Lust doesn't measure up to this definition. In fact, it violates the Bible's definition of love on every count. Using this passage of Scripture as our guide, let's compare God's assessment of love to the devil's counterfeit of lust:

LOVE

1. Love is patient.
2. Love is kind.

LUST

1. Lust can't wait; is impulsive.

LOVE

3. Love does not envy.
4. Love does not boast.
5. Love is not proud.
6. Love is not rude.
7. Love is not self-seeking.
8. Love is not easily angered.
9. Love keeps no record of wrongs.
10. Loves does not delight in evil.
11. Love rejoices in the truth.
12. Love always protects.
13. Love always trusts.
14. Love always hopes.
15. Love always perseveres.
16. Love never fails; it is constant, enduring and faithful to the end.

LUST

2. Lust is cruel, critical and manipulative.
3. Lust seeks more than it earns.
4. Lust builds self at another's expense.
5. Lust is easily threatened.
6. Lust is disrespectful and thoughtless.
7. Lust is demanding and uncaring.
8. Lust is temperamental and retaliates.
9. Lust does not forget offenses.
10. Lust commits wrong to get its own way; rationalizes.
11. Lust encourages lies and covers up misdeeds.
12. Lust takes to gain its own ends and lacks concern for consequences to others.
13. Lust is suspicious and jealous.
14. Lust says one chance and you're out.
15. Lust backs out when it's no longer convenient.
16. Lust ceases when self is no longer served; it is fickle, insecure and unfaithful.

This piece, excerpted from "Is It Love or Lust?" by Dennis Rigstad, was first published in *Psychology for Living* and is used with permission of the Narramore Christian Foundation, Rosemead, Calif. 91770.

FOR FURTHER THOUGHT...

- What about these lists caught your attention?
- The description of lust can be a mirror for you. Where did you see yourself in the list of characteristics?
- Often we think of lust as drooling over Playboy, but there are degrees of lust. What do you do to stop lust when it starts? Do you pray?
- First Corinthians 13 is a description of love and, therefore, a description of Jesus. On which point do you want Jesus to start making you more like Him?
- How can love—as the Bible defines it—help you improve your dating relationships?

????

PART IV

Sex
Keeping a Clear Head
What God Is Saying
People Are Waiting
How Far Is Too Far?

DATING STUFF:

GUYS AND GIRLS

15

Putting the Chill on a Hot Date

We've stressed how important *we* think it is to date friends who live by a value system that is similar to yours.

Yeah, I know. Why have you stressed this so much?

Because if *you're* determined not to go past a kiss and you're dating someone with similar values, it's less likely he/she will pressure you to go farther.

Yeah, but sometimes it happens.

You're right. Sometimes it does. *Sometimes* good Christian kids let down their guard.

So what do I do if I'm on a date and things start to get out of hand?

Good question. For starters, if you're a guy and *she's* too hot to handle, physically force her to stop and say something like, "Excuse me, but I'm not really attracted to girls who throw themselves at me. It makes me wonder at how many other guys you've thrown yourself."

If you're a girl and *he's* making the moves, physically pull away and say, "I'm gonna give you a choice. You can either take me home right now, or you can call my dad and ask him to come get me."

Ooooh.

If you're already too physically involved, let me suggest you ask the following questions of yourself *and* your date.

• Does he like kids?

Nope. Well, if they belong to someone ELSE he can tolerate them for a while.

• Does she wish she were married?

Yeah, she really does. But I kinda think maybe it's just because she hates living at home and wants to get away from her parents.

• Is he ready to be married?

No way! He's always talking about trying to get a college scholarship, what he wants to do in life, how much money he'll make someday. He'd HATE being married right now.

• Is she ready for midnight feedings, changing diapers, runny noses, incessant crying, cooking and cleaning house on a d-a-i-l-y basis?

Are you kidding? She'd flip!

• Is he at a point where he can financially handle

rent, doctors' bills, insurance, possibly working the night shift at any job he can find, putting further schooling on hold?

He'd be totally miserable. I think he'd also feel very trapped and maybe even blame it on me!

• What would her parents say if she told them she was pregnant?

It would KILL them. Not only that, but she'd probably suffer a lot of guilt and shame. My guess? She'd withdraw. OK, if I'm TOTALLY honest, I know it would change her life forever. I mean, she has these really neat goals, you know? Stuff she's been dreaming about for a long time. It would mess all that up.

• What would his parents say if he told them his girlfriend was pregnant?

Ahhh! I don't even wanna THINK about it. They'd be totally crushed. Not only that, but I think he'd feel pretty far from God. OK, if I'm TOTALLY honest, I think it would hinder his relationship with Christ for the rest of his life. Yeah, he knows God forgives, but HE would have an awful hard time forgiving himself.

Wow. Then really, are a few fleeting hot moments of pleasure worth it?

Bottom line: Good choices = good results. Bad choices = bad consequences. Thinking through a list of questions like this can cool a hot evening *very* fast.

Dear Susie:
I just broke up with my boyfriend. He's hurt, confused and now hates me. I want to be his friend but don't know what to do. —Plano, Tex.

Susie: Give him space. Maybe it hurts too much to go from a relationship back to a simple friendship. Continue to be polite, kind and *genuine*. If he says things that hurt you, don't retaliate. Continue to be mature and keep a smile on your face. It may take awhile, but he'll probably come around eventually.

FOR FURTHER THOUGHT...

• What are some other things you can do to cool off a hot date?
• How can dating someone who has similar values and standards help prevent having to chill a hot date?
• Whose responsibility is it to slow things down when they go too fast and too far?
• Girls, at what point would you STOP your date?
• Guys, at what point would you STOP your date?
• What specific steps can you take so you won't get yourself too close to the edge?

????

SOMETHING DIFFERENT

We're not going to do this very often, but we have a couple of really great "longer" stories that illustrate a few of the things we've been talking about. So, if you're into reading, you're going to love these next chapters!

No Strings Attached

Stacy was planning on a quiet
New Year's Eve at home...
until the doorbell rang.

Dad helped Mom into her coat and then turned to me. "You're sure you'll be OK, Stacy?"

I nodded.

"When's Katie coming over?" Mom said.

I looked at my watch. "In about an hour. She said she'd try to be here by 8:00 P.M. at the latest."

Dad smiled his sweet smile—the one that had a little sadness mixed in. "We won't be late."

I had to laugh. "It's New Year's Eve, Daddy. You're *supposed* to be late."

"Well, we'll be back shortly after midnight," Mom said.

With that, they reluctantly took off.

My parents had been concerned about me for the past month. And who could blame them? When Jeff Bolander broke up with me over Thanksgiving vacation, I went out of control. I couldn't eat or sleep, and I cried constantly. For the first few days, I wouldn't even get out of bed or talk to my friends.

Now, a month later, I wasn't much better. I'd see Jeff in the halls at school, and he'd look the other way. I wanted to die right on the spot.

I loved him so much.

STRUNG ALONG

The phone rang. I picked it up in the family room and plopped down onto the sofa. "Hello?"

"Hi, Stacy." Katie's voice.

"Hi," I said. "What's up?"

"Oh, Stacy—guess who just called and asked me out? Alan Martinson! Can you believe it?"

Katie's happiness made me so jealous I wanted to cry. But since everyone was sick of my moping, I determined to put up a brave front. "Terrific," I warbled. "When are you going out with him?"

"Tonight."

"Tonight!" I couldn't believe it. "Katie, how could you accept a date for New Year's Eve *on* New Year's Eve?"

"It's not his fault he had to ask so late," Katie said. "He's been out of town with his folks the whole Christmas vacation. They just got back, and he decided to take a wild chance and see if I might be free."

It sounded phony to me, but I couldn't burst Katie's bubble. "Well, I guess that makes it okay. Where are you going?"

"To Maggie Warren's party. We're doubling with Erin and Tom."

"Sounds great," I said in my cheeriest voice.

"I know I was supposed to spend the evening with you, Stacy. Please understand. *Please.*"

"I understand," I lied. "Have fun."

We told each other good-bye, and almost as soon as I

hung up, the phone rang again. This time it was Erin.

"I'm calling because Tom said we should ask you to come to Maggie's with us. He knows Jeff won't be there, because Jessica Stone broke her date with him. She has the flu. Tom says there'll be other kids at the party without dates. Want to come?"

"Thanks, but no thanks," I said.

"Tom says you shouldn't be alone tonight."

The trouble with talking to Erin is that every other word is *Tom.*

"Look, I appreciate the offer, but I'm fine. OK?"

"You sure?"

"I'm sure. Are you going to wear your new sweater?"

"No. Tom's decided he doesn't like me in blue. Isn't that the pits? Half of my wardrobe is blue, and now I can't wear it."

"Oh, well, you'll manage," I said. "Have fun tonight. Call me tomorrow."

"Will do. Bye."

After Erin hung up, I sat and listened to the dial tone for a moment. Then I banged the phone down on its cradle, startling my cat who was curled up at my feet.

"Sorry, Guinevere," I said and scooped her up onto my lap. She began to purr.

"Guinevere, we girls are a sorry lot," I said. "Did you know that? There's Katie—so eager to go out with Alan she jumps at a last-minute invitation that's downright insulting. And Erin lets Tom tell her *exactly* what she can and can't do and where they'll go. He makes all the decisions."

I sighed. "But who am *I* to talk? When I dated Jeff, he wouldn't let me wear eye shadow. He watched my weight like a hawk and had a fit if I cried at the movies. That's just the way it was. And if he called me right now and asked me to go out with him, I would. In a minute. See what I mean, Guinevere? Katie, Erin and I are like puppets, and the guys are our puppeteers."

Suddenly I began to blubber. "But I miss Jeff so much. What happened? I mean, one minute he was telling me he loved me. Next thing I knew he was telling me that we should start seeing other people. What did I do wrong? Why did he change? And why am I all alone on New Year's Eve?"

I gently pushed the cat to the floor, stood and headed for my room. A crying fit was on the way, and the best place for that was facedown on my bed.

TIED IN KNOTS

Halfway down the hall, I heard the doorbell ring.

Katie? I wondered. *Maybe she changed her mind.*

But when I answered the door, it wasn't Katie standing on my front porch. It was Jeff!

My heart pounded like crazy.

"Hi," he said.

"Hi."

"Can I come in?"

"Sure."

He strode through the door, took off his parka and tossed it on the front-hall table. Then he turned and eyed me the way he used to—head tilting a little to the side, lips slightly parted. Eyes looking full of love.

"I made a mistake, Stacy. I thought I wanted to date other girls, but I don't. I've missed you so much."

He took me in his arms and kissed my mouth—then my swollen eyes and the tears that were trickling down my cheeks. "Tom said your parents were out for the evening."

"Yes," I said. "New Year's Eve party."

He kissed me again, and I thought I'd explode with happiness.

He stopped long enough to whisper in my ear. "I want you back, Stacy."

A fresh flow of tears began, but these were tears of pure joy.

"Don't cry," he murmured. "Everything's fine. I love you."

Another kiss. Oh, how I loved him!

"Let's go to your bedroom," he said.

I was stunned. "You know we can't do that. It's wrong."

He shook his head. "Not for us. Not anymore. Our relationship is for keeps this time, which means it's OK to share our love."

His words were melting my heart. I felt the familiar urges I'd battled when we dated and remembered the temptations. I'd fought them off then, and I *had* to fight them off now.

"Why don't we go to Maggie's party?" I asked.

Jeff rolled his eyes toward the ceiling. "Stacy, we're not going to Maggie's and waste this perfect opportunity. This empty house. A good four hours alone. Who knows when we'll get a chance like this again?"

"Will you come over and watch the Rose Bowl with me tomorrow?" I asked.

"Why this sudden interest in football?"

"I just wanted to know when I'm going to see you again."

His shoulders sagged. "Stacy, you're whining. You know how I hate that."

"I'm sorry," I murmured.

He took my hand and began pulling me down the hallway leading to my room. "Come on. You know you want to."

I felt myself giving in.

Please, dear God, give me the strength to do what's right.

It suddenly occurred to me that the biggest reason I was close to giving in had nothing to do with love. I was afraid of losing him again.

But was he just using *me?* He knew I was all alone tonight. He knew how much I wanted him back. Did he think I'd do anything to make it happen?

"I don't think so," I heard myself say.

"Stacy, I love you. And if you really loved me—"

Something exploded inside me. "If I really loved you? Jeff, everyone in the entire school knows I love you! I've been walking around there for over a month with red, swollen eyes and a tear-stained face. My pride is shot. My grades have dropped out of sight. Of course I love you. But I don't think it's fair for you to spring back into my life like this and expect me to—"

He took me into his arms again. "Don't you see, Babe? This night was meant to be. Everything is perfect. So, are you serious about this reconciliation or not?"

"I'm serious. It's just that—"

"Do we go to your bedroom? Yes or no, Stacy?"

"No," I said in a voice so small I hardly recognized it as my own.

"I'm leaving then."

I nodded.

He shook his head. "I can't believe this." He spun on his heel and marched back down the hallway. After a few seconds, I heard the door open and then close again.

THE FINAL TUG

I panicked. *You've blown your only chance to get him back! Go after him!*

But I stood stock-still. Guinevere rubbed against my leg. Feeling totally drained, I sat down on the floor beside her.

After a while, I began stroking her back.

"You know, Kitty, I prayed for strength to do the right thing, and God gave it to me. But I want Jeff back so much. Maybe I'll call him tomorrow and—"

I sprang to my feet. "No! If I get back with Jeff, I'll wind up being his puppet all over again. I've got to start being my own person."

I flipped my arms up and down.

"Look, Guinevere, I can move my arms all by myself. No strings attached!"

I headed for the kitchen with the cat at my heels.

"I think I'll make some cookies," I said. "Then I'm going to put a sad movie in the VCR, watch it, eat cookies and cry my eyes out. Loud. As loud as I can. Isn't it amazing, Guinevere? Not only can I move without strings, I can even make my own decisions."

My cat jumped up on the counter, watching me as I began to make the cookies.

I giggled as I measured the flour. "Guinevere, there's good news and bad news. The bad news is that I'm all alone on New Year's Eve, boring you to death with my rambling. The good news is that I'm making progress. I'm starting to do my own thing. Tomorrow I'm going to the store and buy every shade of eye shadow I can find! And that, Guinevere, is just the beginning."

By Susan C. Hall, a freelance writer from Rockford, Ill. This story first appeared in a special abstinence issue of *Brio/Breakaway* magazine, November 1993.

That's one smart cookie!

Creative Ideas to Keep Your Mind Headed in the Right Direction

• Pray for your future husband or wife every night. Ask God to keep them from temptation, keep them pure, make them into the man/woman of God that you need and give them a strong desire to obey Jesus Christ.

• Decide the stopping point so, in the heat of the moment, there is never a choice of whether to continue or stop. Have both of you commit to it, perhaps even sign a card. Write it in a place you'll see it, such as inside the back page of your Bible. If the options are taken away, the decision will be much easier to follow.

• Memorize 1 Corinthians 6:20: "You were bought at a price. Therefore honor God with your body." Remember that the next time your hormones tell you something your mind doesn't want to do.

Hey Greg:

I have a big problem. I can't keep my mind off sex. I'll be sitting in class and my mind suddenly goes haywire. I've heard it's normal for guys, but is it normal for a Christian guy? Isn't it sinful? How do I stop? —Lancaster, Pa.

GREG: Even if you were locked up in a backwoods cabin in Albania, sexual thoughts would still likely enter your head. It's normal to have sexual thoughts, but it's what we do with them that makes them wrong.

At one time or another in their lives, most people have thought what it would be like to hurt someone. Is it a sin to think about hurting someone for a few seconds and then dismiss it? Only if you begin to devise a plan to actually do something about it and then follow through with that plan.

Sexual images bombard us. They are on billboards, commercials and magazine ads. When someone wants to sell something, they'll usually use sex to sell it. I once saw an ad for a chain saw held by a girl in a bikini. What does a scantily clad female in a dark forest have to do with chain saws? Nothing. But the advertiser's goal was to get my attention. It worked—though I didn't buy their chain saw!

When sexual thoughts enter our brain, we have two choices: (a) take those thoughts captive and kick them out as 2 Corinthians 10:5 says to do, or (b) dwell on them, toy with them and allow them to take root in our brain so they can visit us again.

It takes practice to kick out those thoughts, especially if we believe they're "just thoughts." It's true, one thought doesn't lead to an action that would betray our faith, but thoughts left unchecked over several years—or even weeks—soon result in an action. And guess what? Actions become habits, and habits often shape our destiny. That's Satan's strategy. If he can get young guys to dwell on sex, he knows they'll want to act on their thoughts sooner or later. It's an intense battle that many guys are losing.

Ask anyone who has engaged in sexual promiscuity or sexual perversion and they will readily admit: *If I just could have checked my thoughts earlier in life, I wouldn't have done the things I did.*

The best way to overcome a haywire head is to replace unhealthy lies *("Girls like to be used.")* with truth. I suggest you memorize at least two of the following verses so you can start to quote them whenever your brain is attacked with sexual thoughts.

> Submit yourselves, then, to God. Resist the devil, and he will flee from you. Come near to God and he will come near to you (Jas. 4:7,8).

> No temptation has seized you except what is common to man. And God is faithful; he will not let you be tempted beyond what you can bear. But when you are tempted, he will also provide a way out so that you can stand up under it (1 Cor. 10:13).

> I can do everything through him who gives me strength (Phil. 4:13.

> Because he himself suffered when he was tempted, he is able to help those who are being tempted (Heb. 2:18).

> Clothe yourselves with the Lord Jesus Christ, and do not think about how to gratify the desires of the sinful nature (Rom. 13:14).

• Though it's tough if the physical dominoes have fallen, put them back up. That is, reverse the trend of going farther sexually each time you're together. If both of you can recall how easy the dominoes fall, it won't be just one person trying to pour cold water on a heated moment.

• **Guys:** Keep an image of your future bride dressed in white and walking down the aisle of the church. To look at her and know that she is unstained by you or others is the greatest feeling in the world. Do not violate your dream or the dream some other guy could have had with your girl (in case you do not marry her).

• Girls: Hold tight to the goal of having a clean conscience when you walk down the aisle dressed in white. Look forward to the day when you can walk down that aisle, look into the eyes of your future lifetime husband, and know that he will be yours alone.

• Realize there is a 98 percent chance you will *never* marry the person you date in high school.

• Premarital sex breaks up more dating couples than any other factor.

• It's difficult to forget previous sexual partners. Once you are married, it's difficult not to compare them to your mate.

• Ask yourself, *Will I find it difficult to trust my future mate if I know that he/she was sexually experienced before marriage? If he/she did it once, could he/she do it again with someone else if the circumstances were right?*

• Realize this fact: Persons and couples who have premarital sex are more likely to have extramarital affairs as well.

• Pleasure can blind. Premarital sex often fools a person into marrying someone who really isn't right for them.

• Love is a decision, not a feeling. The most loving decision you can make when your mind tells you it wants sex is to say no.

FOR FURTHER THOUGHT...
- What do you think about praying for your future husband/wife? When did you, or will you, start?
- What other words of wisdom from friends, the Bible, your youth pastor or someone you respect can help remind you to stay pure until marriage?
- Who do you have praying for you and your dating? Or who can you ask to pray for you and hold you accountable?

????

Everyone's Doing It?

Now that you're into the guy/girl thing, you're likely in one of three places: You are (A) saving your virginity for marriage, (B) involved in sexual relations and have no plans to stop, or (C) trying to make a new start. You've had sex but got hurt and now want to save yourself till marriage.

If you answered A or C, you've made an extremely *wise* and *mature* decision. You're using your *head* instead of your *hormones* to determine your choices. And though you may feel lonely at times, you are *not* alone!

Here are a few examples of some people you may recognize who do believe in the importance of sexual purity.

DAVID ROBINSON, SAN ANTONIO SPURS CENTER:

"Too many people think, *Well, I'm not going to abstain from sex, so I'll just try 'safe sex.'* But you have a choice to make, and if you make the wrong choice, you're going to have to suffer the consequences. As a Christian, I'm not accepting anything less than God's best."

KIRK CAMERON, ACTOR:

"It's easy to look at life as a great ride or an awesome game and decide that you're out to have as much fun as you can. And some people see sex that way. But a condom can't protect you from a broken heart. Sex within marriage is the only kind that's truly fun and exciting—the kind that lasts for a lifetime. I'm glad I waited."

TOBY MCKEEHAN, DC TALK, MUSICIAN:

"Each of us in DC Talk has chosen not to believe the lie of 'safe sex.' Some of our friends, on the other hand, did buy the lie. Now they have miserable lives...and aren't able to pursue their dreams."

HORACE GRANT, CHICAGO BULLS FORWARD:

"God's been trying to tell us since the dawn of time, since He created the world, this important message: Sexual immorality is not the way to go. The best safe sex is not to have sex, except with your wife."

DARIUS MCCRARY, ACTOR ON *FAMILY MATTERS*:

"I'm saving myself for my future wife because that's what I believe is right. It has nothing to do with being a TV star. It's all about respect—for myself and the person I plan to marry."

DAVE DRAVECKY, FORMER SAN FRANCISCO GIANTS PITCHER:

"From my experience, there's a precious value in a relationship with one woman—your wife. Until you get married, run away from temptation as if Freddy Krueger is two steps behind you. Abstinence can save your life."

KEVIN JOHNSON, PHOENIX SUNS POINT GUARD:

"Look at Magic Johnson's situation. Now he's telling people, 'It's cool to be a virgin. The mistake I made is life threatening. Don't make that mistake.'"

OREL HERSHISER, LOS ANGELES DODGERS PITCHER:

"If you've been sexually active, it's not too late to start over. You can be self-controlled and have your dignity back. You *can* become abstinent from this point forward."

CANDACE CAMERON, ACTRESS ON *FULL HOUSE:*

"Since sex is such a unique gift, I don't want to share it with a bunch of people. This is something I want to experience with one person and one person only. So I'm waiting till marriage."

NEW BEGINNINGS

OK, you're thinking. *So, not everyone's doing it. But I've already established my dating reputation. To change my actions would demand a rethinking of my entire dating life!*

Hmmm. And maybe that's not such a bad idea. I mean, if you really love yourself, wouldn't you want the best for *you?* So let's talk about dating and some ideas that are so ancient they might seem brand new.

Old/New Idea 1: You don't have to kiss a guy on the first date. Maybe you're thinking, *Kiss? I'm battling with whether or not to have sex with a guy on the first date!* OK, so let's go in reverse for a second. *Lots* of people don't even *kiss* on the first date. As soon as a guy and girl get physically involved (on ANY level) it bonds them closer together. We're talking first date here. You're probably not even sure you *want* to be bonded with this guy yet. So take a deep breath and just back off when he moves forward.

Dear Susie:

My boyfriend wants to have sex. So do I, but I know it's wrong. What if I'm drunk? Will I be able to resist him again? —Detroit, Mich.

Susie: No, you probably won't. Why are you even asking, "If I'm drunk?" *Plan not to be!* God wants you to be in control of your body. If you're messing around with alcohol, you're *not* in control and are farther away from Him than you realize.

I'm guessing you're throwing yourself into the party scene. Wake up! Step back from such close relationships with non-Christians who are pressuring you to go against God's will.

I'm glad you know that having sex with your boyfriend is wrong. Now, do something about it.

Old/New Idea 2: Stay away from an empty house. Your parents are out for the evening—or *his* parents are gone for the weekend. Decision: Are you going to spend time together in an empty house with empty beds? If so, you're setting yourself up. The temptation is too great.

Old/New Idea 3: Spend more time together in groups. Go out with several couples. Stay in public. Dare to be a little crazy. Pick up a bucket of chicken and go to the airport. Spread a blanket in one of the concourses and have a picnic. Or go to a park and swing, build sand castles and race up the jungle bars. You'll face a lot less temptation having creative fun in a large group.

Old/New Idea 4: Choose your dates carefully. Be selective about whom you go out with. Strive to date guys who hold values similar to your own. You don't drink? Refuse to date guys who do. Good grades are important to you? Then you probably won't be happy dating a guy who ditches, cheats and hates school. Your family places a high priority on church involvement? Look for guys with similar standards—young men who go to church and profess a religious commitment.

Bottom Line: Don't be pressured into having sex. Not only can it be physically and emotionally lethal, but it robs you of the most valuable gift you can present to your future husband. And if you've already lost your virginity, realize that *you* are in charge of the future. Make some strong decisions *now* to determine your future sexuality. Dare to take a stand. You're not alone! I promise.

Portions of this chapter first appeared in a special abstinence issue of *Brio/Breakaway,* November 1993.

Hey Greg:
One of my best friends is in a relationship with this girl. He doesn't talk a lot about it, but he has told me how far they've gone (too far). He's totally changed. It's like he can't think about anything else except her. He doesn't call me or the guys anymore, and his grades are going down. What should I do? —Elkhart, Ind.

GREG: If he were *my* friend, and he'd gone through that much of a behavior shift, this is what I'd do: First, I'd take him out to lunch or go over to his house where we could talk privately. Then I'd calmly tell him the facts as I see them, all the while reaffirming my loyalty and friendship for him. I'd want him to see that my motives aren't to break up him and this girl (though that's probably what needs to happen), but to express my concern and see if I have the facts straight.

My goal is to get him to agree with my conclusions that his life is WAY out of balance. If he doesn't agree, lust has probably blinded him to the truth. Has he gone off the deep end? Perhaps. If so, then it's important to stay in contact with him, letting him know you'll be there no matter what. Eventually, he's going to need a friend to help pick up the pieces when the relationship ends—and 99.5 percent of the time it *will* end. He won't need "I told you so's" either.

To be honest, guy/girl relationships can easily get out of hand during the high school years. Experiencing intense feelings for someone for the first time is something new. Not everyone is mature enough to see the big picture of what going too far and neglecting friends and studies can do. Stick with him and pray for him. He needs a friend like you.

FOR FURTHER THOUGHT...

- Do you ever feel like you're standing alone as it relates to sexual purity?
- Does knowing that others are sticking to their standards help you stick with yours?
- Where can you find others who are committed to sexual purity?

????

"It's Not Funny, God!"

We've met a few teens who have wanted to have a face-to-face conversation with God on the subject of love and sex—and they weren't always happy with Him! What are they feeling? What would they like to say? Perhaps something like this:

Do You like sick jokes or something? First, You create me. That's cool, because it's nice to be alive. But then You put people of the opposite sex all around me. What am I supposed to do, not look at them? Because sometimes when I do, my mind has a tendency to go wacko. What can I say? I'm attracted to them. Not only do I like what I see, I want to get to know them. I want to talk, look at, touch...I want to love someone and have someone love me. And once I get to the love stage, that's when things start to get totally UN-funny! My feelings get carried away. It's like I can't help it.

I don't care whether some people think it's puppy love or hamster love—it's real. And my mind wants to do more than hold hands; it wants to touch in places that make us both feel good. But just because I'm one of Your followers—

a Christian—I'm told I can't! Aaaahhhhh! Why did You create me, give me these emotions, put someone I really care for in my life...and then say, "Not until you're married, nyah, nyah, nyah, nyah, nyah, nyah"? Do You like sick jokes, or something?

Though God doesn't actually have to respond to that type of tirade (as honest as it is), let's pretend He does. What would He say? Something like this?

Got you again! Ha, ha, I just love being God. First, I get to make you. Then I get to watch you scrape your knees on the playground and break your arms on the monkey bars—then the REAL fun begins.

You see, what I did was make you so your hormones start doing weird things at about age 11 or 12. Not only do I change your bodies so half the time you feel rotten about yourself, I try to make the opposite sex very intriguing to you. Then, when you start getting interested in someone—and maybe fall in love—that's when I have the pleasure of totally frustrating you. Your mind tells you how fun it would be to go exploring...and do a few other things only grown-ups should do, but I've got this big black book that tells you to wait until you're married! What a joke. You should see the look on your face when I nudge your conscience and remind you of how evil and sinful you are.

Yep, it sure is fun being God—especially the part where people are mad at Me all the time for making them attracted to the opposite sex.

Or would He say something like this?

Thanks for being honest with Me! You don't know how much I appreciate it when people say what they feel. It doesn't make Me mad...really!

I completely understand your frustration. But put yourself in *My* shoes for a second. I had kind of a dilemma when I created males and females. I needed them to populate the earth, so I thought up the idea of sex. Think about it. How populated do you think the world would be if a man and woman weren't attracted to each other? You're right. Not very. And I'd still be playing three-handed pinochle with Adam and Eve.

So I had to put something inside to awaken them to each other. And I couldn't just make the time bomb go off at 21. It has to happen slowly.

No, I don't think the problem is the hormones I've given you. (Believe Me, you'll thank Me for them later.) The problem is when should you put them to use.

If you start using them at age 13, who's going to take care of the kid? Oh, I know you *think* your technology has solved that one with pills, and implants, and latex condoms, but it really hasn't. Why? Because I've put something within you that can't be satisfied by simply completing a sex act. Deep within you is a need for real intimacy with another human being. And I've decided that the best place to share that intimate relationship is in the lifetime commitment of marriage. Does that really make me a bad Guy?

OK, enough of putting words into God's mouth. We think you get the drift. God's not a practical joker trying to frustrate you into hating Him. He's really a good God who only wants the absolute, number one best for you—especially when it's something as important as your relationships with the opposite sex.

God Has Feelings

Did you know God has a heart?

Well, maybe it's not the blood-pumping variety we have, but it's certainly something capable of breaking. How do we know? Well, when Mary, the sister of Lazarus, got on Jesus' case for being late to the "brother raising," He was deeply moved and troubled (see John 11:17-37). Though she had known Jesus for a long time, she still hadn't learned to trust Him. Plus, a bunch of other people got on His case, too. That hurt! And before He proved to them He really knew what He was doing by raising Lazarus back to life, He cried real tears.

People didn't understand what He was doing back then, and some still don't understand. The perfect example is teens like you not always knowing why you're allowed to have intense feelings for the opposite sex—and then not being able to act on them the way your mind and body want.

When the choice is made to get on God's case or ignore His ideal, His heart feels it. Being misunderstood and seeing Your creation go down the wrong path isn't pleasant.

We humans do tons of other things that break His heart, but probably few that bring Him to tears more than the misuse of one of His greatest inventions—the love between a man and a woman.

Think about what God's up against.

• God didn't create this sinful world that isn't interested in following His Word, but He has chosen to stand by it. Sadly, we've reduced a wonderfully made female to an object of men's pleasures. Movies, TV, music and pornographic magazines continually reinforce the idea that women aren't to be respected, but used. Few of these media portray sex as special. Instead, it's cheap and easy—and should be available whenever the urge arises. Did God create that? Can He keep EVERY guy and girl from those influences that definitely are NOT giving the whole story on how guy/girl relationships are *really* supposed to happen?

The answer to both questions is no. Why? He won't put the world on a string. He loves people too much to make them robots.

Next to dying on a cross, the highest form of love God showed us was when He gave us a free will. He respects us enough to allow us to love Him or leave Him, obey *Him* or follow *our* emotions. He knew that if we returned His great love for us out of fear or manipulation, it wouldn't be satisfying.

• God didn't create the public school system with all of the pressure it contains.

For you girls, there's the pressure to date popular guys in order to feel good about yourselves or to fit in with a specific group of friends.

For you guys there's the pressure to go exploring in order to show your friends you're not a dork around girls.

• God didn't create the one-on-one dating structure with all of the temptations it offers. For centuries, young adults your age rarely had the chance to be alone with each other until their wedding night! That was far from the case when your parents were teenagers, and it's WAY far from the case today.

When you put hundreds of teenagers together for eight hours a day in a closed setting, you're going to have girls and guys attracted to each other. With attraction comes a desire to spend time with them. Time alone together brings temptation. Temptation often leads to failure. Failure and sin have consequences—guilt, damaged lives and sometimes babies.

It's after they've blown it once that many teens throw in the towel on trying to stay pure. They get frustrated with God for allowing them to fail.

What will you do when or if you face that frustration and guilt?

Because guilty feelings aren't pleasant, it can cause us to do one of two things:

1. Bury it. Deny you've done anything wrong. Then confirm in your heart that what you're doing is OK and repeat the same mistake over and over.

2. Confess it. This is God's remedy. Admit your mistakes to Him, learn from them and then move on. There is NO LIMIT to how many times you can receive freedom from past mistakes. Although it gets old asking forgiveness for the same mistake, God never grows weary hearing words from a heart that is *genuinely* sorry and wants to try to do better. (The key phrase here is *genuinely sorry.* His willingness to forgive isn't a ticket to do what you want. You shouldn't think, *Ahh, He'll forgive me.* That's not being genuine with your Creator. And that cheapens His forgiveness.)

Which of these two options actually gets rid of the guilt? The first only submerges it, the second removes it completely. Really! (see Psalm 103:9-14). And if you *memorize* it we'll hang your pix on our bulletin board.

PLACING THE BLAME

Although it's our nature to want to put the blame on someone (usually not ourselves), let's review the facts and see if that's really the adult way to handle this dilemma.

1. God created you to be attracted to the opposite sex.

2. You're glad He did.

3. God wants the best for you, so He says to wait until marriage to go exploring sexually.

4. That's not what most of the outside influences in your life are communicating. In fact, the pressure to NOT follow God's standards can sometimes be pretty intense.

5. You're stuck in a school system with dating customs that don't lend themselves to sticking with God's best (though it is certainly not an impossible task).

6. Dealing with failure gets old. And it's often "easier" to cave in and forget about seeking God's help in staying pure.

What we have here is a situation where it's not God's fault for creating in you a desire for the opposite sex, but it's not your fault for living in a culture that puts you in tough situations and even encourages you to do what comes naturally.

Man!

Because neither you nor God is at fault, how can you work together to do things right with the opposite sex?

1. God will do His part when you ask Him for help.

2. You need to know how and when to say no when things could get out of control. (More on this in the next chapter.)

FOR FURTHER THOUGHT...

- Do you understand the dilemma God your Creator is in when it comes to your attraction to the opposite sex? Explain it in your own words.
- Do you think God understands your dilemma when it comes to hormones, attraction and His standards?
- How can you and God work together to pursue His absolute best for you?
- Why did God give us the ability to feel guilty? What do you do with guilt?

????

"When Should I Say No?"

When *should* you say no?

OK, let's practice. I'll give you a few setups. *You* decide when and how "no" should have been said and what consequences each person will face.

1: Marijean is in the eighth grade. She and her boyfriend, Robbie, have been together for two months. Marijean is invited to a slumber party one of her school friends is having. Though Marijean is a Christian, none of her friends at the party are.

After the parents have gone to bed, the girls sneak some beer from the fridge. Marijean has never tasted beer before and, as everyone else is drinking, she feels pressured to try it. She doesn't get drunk, but she *does* get woozy.

Later, the girls start calling guys on the telephone. Marijean calls Robbie and invites him to come over. When he arrives, she sneaks out of the house in her flimsy nightgown. She's still a little ditzy from the beer and her inhibitions are down. She and Robbie start making out and eventually have sex.

• *What consequences will Marijean face? Robbie?*
• *How will this affect her "Christian witness" to her non-Christian friends?*
• *When and how should Marijean have said no?*

2: Dave and Sandi are both high school juniors and have been dating for three months. They go to the same church and are involved in their youth group. Dave picks up Sandi for a typical Friday night date. They go to their school football game together and then hit the local pizza hangout afterward.

It's crowded when they arrive, so Dave suggests they grab a pizza to go and take it home to share with his folks. When Sandi and Dave arrive at his house, he finds a note from his parents saying they decided to go out for the evening with another couple from church. It's 10:00 P.M. According to the message, they won't be back until 11:30 P.M.

Dave flips on the TV and pours Sandi a Coke. They scarf the pizza and then sit on the couch to watch a late-night movie together. Sandi feels safe and secure in Dave's arms and eventually rests her head on his shoulders. Thirty minutes later they're stretched out on the couch. It's 11:00 P.M. Dave has been stroking her hair, arms and face with his hands. He eventually leans over to kiss her and rolls on top of her.

Sandi's heart is racing. *He shouldn't be on top of me!* she thinks. *But it feels so good.* His hands slip underneath her sweater. Five minutes later, nearly nude, they're glued together side by side. Suddenly, the door opens. Yep, Dave's parents are home early.

• *What consequences will Dave face? Sandi?*
• *How will this affect their future dates with each other?*
• *When and how should they have said no?*

3: Even though Josh is a ninth-grader, he could easily pass for a 17-year-old. His weight training and athletic involvement have paid off—he's solid, muscular and confident.

During the summer, he and his family travel 10 hours to spend two weeks in a rented beach house. Josh is excited because he loves the water and everything about it—fishing, snorkeling, swimming, bodysurfing...you name it.

Jodi, an 18-year-old, just-graduated high school senior, has been watching him from a distance. She's a local who is working at the concession stand at the beach this particular summer. She just ended a one-year relationship with Brad...and, yes, they were sexually active.

She's feeling vulnerable now and wants a summer fling before she heads off to college. Josh is looking pretty good.

He's never even had a girlfriend. Lots of girls have chased him, but he's always been too involved in sports to go out with anyone.

Later that evening, Jodi approaches him. She compliments his athletic ability, mentions that she's been watching him for a week now, and guesses there's nothing he can't do in the water.

This makes Josh feel great—especially when he finds out she's an older woman! She tells him how attracted to him she feels and asks if he wants to meet her for a late-night walk along the beach.

Later that night, Josh sneaks out of the beach house and meets Jodi. She takes his hand and leads him along the beach, continuing to tell him how good-looking and strong he is.

About 20 minutes later, Jodi says she's cold and asks Josh to build a small fire in a secluded area. He does, and they snuggle next to the flames. Jodi runs her hands through his hair, then starts unbuttoning his shirt. He feels strange—guilty and excited—all at the same time.

I know this is wrong, he thinks, *but I don't wanna stop. Besides, I'm afraid she'll know I'm inexperienced with girls if I start backing off.*

Josh has sex for the first time, and Jodi leaves the next day for college.

• *What consequences will Josh face? Jodi?*

• *Josh hasn't even started dating yet. Will this affect his first relationship? If so, how?*

• *Jodi has been sexually active, but she didn't bother to tell Josh. What could result?*

• *As this was Josh's first time to have sex, and he's never had a girlfriend, we can assume he was unprotected. Discuss what may happen as a result.*

• *When and how should they have said no?*

Dear Susie:

My boyfriend likes to stroke my legs from knee to midthigh. It makes me uncomfortable. What should I do? —Little Rock, Ark.

Susie: What you've described is known as "petting." The Holy Spirit works through our conscience to help us feel guilty when we're involved in things we shouldn't do. You're uncomfortable for a good reason: Petting can escalate to sexual intercourse and, therefore, should be saved for marriage.

Once the engine is revved and speeding uphill, it's awfully hard to slow down and put things in reverse. Tell this guy you're not going to let him do this anymore. If he respects your decision and likes you enough to honor that, fine. If not, break up fast!

FOR FURTHER THOUGHT...

- What makes saying no hard?
- Is it easier to say no to circumstances than to people? Explain what circumstances it is good to say no to.
- We've looked at consequences for not saying no. What are the good consequences—the benefits—of saying no?

????

Trains, Watches...and Automobiles

The moonlight was golden, and I'd just pulled Jenny close when she yelled, "Ow! My hair."

Her head was cocked at an awkward angle. I leaned forward to peek around her right ear and saw a great wad of her beautiful blond hair caught in my watchband. I was ticked. Our moment was shattered.

"Hold still, Jenny. I'll get it."

"Ow. Dean, it hurts!"

I slipped the watch off my wrist and let her deal with the tangled mess.

"Nice watch," she commented halfheartedly. "Where'd you get it?"

It was an innocent question that took my mind back to a night four years earlier. I'd turned 13 that night, and instead of the usual family dinner at home, Dad had whisked me off to an incredible restaurant.

* * *

Being surprised is always nice, but it also makes me feel uneasy and kinda suspicious. Dad had never done anything like this before, and I wondered what the evening would hold.

I looked at the menu. "Dad," I whispered, "what should I get? Look at the prices!"

"Anything you want."

"Anything?"

I looked at the menu. Frog Legs...nah. I might have been 13, but I still wouldn't eat a frog. After all, just a few years ago they were my friends who lived down at Brown's pond.

"*Hummm*, Soft-Shell Crab—Cajun Style."

Living in New Orleans had its advantages, and one of them was the terrific food. I finally chose Gumbo Ya-Ya and Cajun Shrimp...what a meal! But what happened between Dad and me was even better than the food.

"Dean," he said, "you're heading into some of the most important years of your life."

I looked up and saw that serious look on his face.

"The choices you make during your teen years can help make your life satisfying and successful, or they can destroy you. One of the most important and most difficult relates to sex."

I tried to look cool, nonchalant. Dad said that word right out loud like you'd say "pizza" or something. I nodded, picturing a large pizza, loaded with pepperoni and sausage. It was a familiar thought that made me feel more comfortable. But my face was hot, and I began to sweat. (Cajun Shrimp is pretty spicy.)

Dad continued, "It's kind of like a train."

Oh good, back in safe territory. I could deal with trains.

"Say you and a group of others are at a train station, Dean."

"Yeah?"

"And every one of you has a ticket for the train."

"Where's the train going?"

"That depends on you."

(This sounded like one of Dad's famous needle stories. He'd tell them to my brothers and me and then ask, "Get the point?")

"See, Dean, this is the fastest, most powerful train in the world. When you get on, you'll get the ride of your life. And if you make the right choice, you can ride it over and over again."

"Hey, Dad," I whispered, "what's this got to do with, ummm, that other thing?"

"Sex?"

"Shh!"

"Oh, sorry son." He lowered his voice a bit. "Here's the connection. Each ticket has a specific boarding time. If you get on at the wrong time, you end up in the wrong place. Like Tom."

"Tom?"

"Yeah, he's a kid who watched as others got on the train. He saw the look of pleasure on their faces and heard the excitement in their voices. They urged him to join them. He stood for a while, waiting for his appointed boarding time. But he was too impatient. He was the kind who wanted what he wanted when *he* wanted it. He got tired of waiting and got on the train early, before the appointed time."

"So the trip was a dud?"

"No, he loved the trip."

"So?"

"But he ended up at the wrong destination."

"Where?"

"Death."

"What?"

"Well, Proverbs says that the path of the prostitute leads to death."

"Prostitutes?"

"Yeah, Dean. A prostitute is a person who—"

"I know, Dad, but what's a prostitute have to do with the train?"

He raised his left eyebrow, which meant he didn't quite follow me. I leaned forward.

"What's the prostitute have to do with sex?"

He raised his right eyebrow and looked at me weird.

"Umm," I tried again, "what I mean is, with the train and all of that."

"It's all sex outside of marriage. In Proverbs it says (Dad's voice grew dramatic), '...she seduced him with her smooth talk. All at once he followed her like an ox going to the slaughter, like a deer stepping into a noose 'til an arrow pierces his liver....Her house is a highway to the grave, leading down to the chambers of death.'" His voice was very low and very deep when he finished.

"It says *that* in the Bible?"

"In Proverbs 7. Boy, this rice tastes great!" he said to cut the tension.

"Dad," I asked with genuine concern, "do you feel OK?"

"Sure, Dean. Do you feel OK?"

"I mean, you're not making much sense."

"Listen, sex will be the single most repeatable pleasure in your life—if you wait for God's timing. He's planned the time for you to board the train. And that time is on your wedding night. Then you and your wife can ride that train over and over and enjoy arriving at the destination together."

"Where's that?"

"Though you probably don't care too much for it now, it's the place of intimacy and total trust. The place where love is shared freely and two people become one. The trip itself is different for each couple and, believe me, it gets better as time goes on."

My dad's eyes were shining softly. I knew what he was thinking.

"Like you and Mom?"

He nodded. "Waiting for your mother was one of the best and most important decisions I ever made. It formed the foundation for our marriage. It wasn't always easy, Dean. In fact, it was never very easy because I'd heard about that train and what a great ride it offered and because she's so beautiful. But, timing has everything to do with sex. And sex has everything to do with timing. If you're unmarried, it's not time to get on the train. Get the point?"

"Yeah, Dad, I get it."

"Happy birthday, Dean. This is to remind you to wait for God's timing."

That's when I opened the foil-wrapped package that held my watch. I wear it every day. It reminds me of the commitment I made that night on my 13th birthday. I decided to wait until the right time to board the train and to reach the destination with my future wife.

Now with Jenny cuddled next to me, her hair caught in my watchband, I remembered my promise, and answered her question.

"My dad gave it to me on my 13th birthday."

"Did he know it could get caught in a girl's hair?"

"Sure, Jenny," I said with a shrug, "that's one of the reasons he gave it to me. Hey, why don't we grab a burger? I'm hungry."

Sue Cameron is a freelance writer living in Texas. This article first appeared in the August 1992 issue of *Breakaway*.

Greg and I hope you're as determined to wait as Dean is. Of course, it's not necessary that you have a physical reminder (like a watch) to help you keep your commitment. Your promise to God is the most important factor.

But if you *do* want a physical reminder, you can use other things besides a watch.

Meet Michelle Stevens. She's a 16-year-old who is also committed to maintaining her virginity.

"When I turned 13," she explains, "my dad took me on my first date. It was really fun. We both got dressed up, he opened all the doors for me, and we went to one of the best restaurants in town.

"That's when he presented me with the Love Pendant. And like the dad in this story, he explained that when I started dating, he and my mom expected me to stick with God's plan for sexual purity."

Are you familiar with the Love Pendant? It's a gold necklace displaying three question marks. Each one symbolizes an important facet of your decision. The questions? "Am I maintaining my sexual purity as a commitment to God? My parents? Myself?"

Michelle loves her gift so much that she saved up her money and bought two for her closest girlfriends who are also determined to wait until marriage.

"It's really neat," Michelle says. "All three of us wear them to school and lots of people ask us about them. Everyone especially wants to know what the question marks mean. It's a great way to share my beliefs with others without being preachy."

When Michelle's brother turned 13, his mom took him on a special mom-son weekend trip and presented him with the same challenge. His chastity reminder? A watch—just like Dean's—that he loves to wear.

✳   ✳   ✳

Many parents have presented their sons and daughters with gold key chains, rings, watches or necklaces to serve as reminders that sexual purity until marriage is the choice God wants them to make.

How can I get my parents to give me something to remind me of my commitment to remain sexually pure?

Ask your mom and dad if you can set aside a few uninterrupted moments to talk with them about something very important. When that time arrives, express your desire to follow God's will for your life and tell them you want to keep your virginity until marriage.

Explain what you've read (or show them this chapter) and ask if they would consider giving you a chastity symbol as a gift.

If they choose not to be a part of this venture, then see if you can line up a few extra baby-sitting jobs or a paper route and purchase your own. And find another adult to pray for you and encourage you (a youth leader, pastor, coach).

Above all, remember it's not the *physical* item that's important; it's your *spiritual* commitment to your heavenly Father.

(If you're interested in ordering the Love Pendant for $19.99, call Focus on the Family at 1-800-232-6459. Ask for item TX054.)

FOR FURTHER THOUGHT...

- Look again at the story Dean's dad told him. What did you learn from the train story? What did it help you understand better?

- How does/would a physical reminder of your commitment to stay sexually pure help you to keep that commitment?

- Will you want to take your son/daughter on their first date as Dean's dad and Michelle's dad did? Why would this be important?

????

On a Road to Nowhere

True story of a good girl
who let down her guard.

Heather* is exceptionally pretty when she laughs. Her smile leaps across her face, forcing double dimples, and her green eyes sparkle. There are moments, however, when her eyes become dull and her shoulders slump—signs that she's still reeling from a painful blow.

When I was growing up, I didn't have much to worry about. I had a healthy relationship with my parents, was self-confident and felt strong in my religious convictions. And I knew there were things you just didn't do.

I was involved in a ton of activities with the youth group, friends and sports—especially soccer. Being small didn't stop me from playing tough in the game, and I was good enough to make it on the championship high school team.

(*Names have been changed.)

Heather's happy, carefree life seemed to become even brighter near the beginning of her junior year, when she met Steve.

Everything was great at the start of our relationship. We talked a lot, laughed together and had very little physical contact. My parents liked Steve, too, which was important to me.

But then he started to get possessive. He was jealous of soccer, my family, my friends. He wanted to be the center of my life, so he began to manipulate me. He became very sarcastic and started slamming my religious convictions. I began questioning everything I believed in. He knew just what strings to pull, and I let him dominate my life.

When summer came, we spent way too much time together. We'd go to his house or mine when our parents weren't home. Every time we were alone, our physical limits were pushed a little further.

Wrong Turn

One day, while we were messing around, he held me down, completely ignoring me when I told him I didn't want to have sex. I should have shoved him off and run, but I didn't. I remember thinking to myself, *I've let him go this far. I don't have the right to stop him now.*

I went ahead with it, but afterward I felt awful. I'd always said I was saving myself for marriage.

After that first time, Steve expected Heather to have sex with him frequently.

I know now that if you're doing something wrong and you want to quit, you *can*. But my self-esteem was so low at that point I thought I *had* to stay with Steve because no other guy would be interested in me.

My parents saw how unhappy and depressed I'd

become and tried to talk with me about it. They finally stopped allowing me to see Steve. But by this time he had such control over me that I ignored Mom and Dad. I continued to see him secretly, in spite of their warnings.

Finally, after Christmas her senior year, Heather's best friend, Molly, confronted her.

"Heather," she said, "this is getting ridiculous! You used to be happy—always smiling and positive, never a thing wrong. Now you're constantly down— you just sit there and 'veg.' WAKE UP!"

What Molly said hit me like a brick! She gave me the courage I needed to break up with Steve.

AN UNEXPECTED CURVE

Heather was headed in the right direction...until she agreed to go with Steve to the senior prom. She jumped right back onto the same physical and emotional roller coaster. Two weeks later, Heather became pregnant.

Up to this point, she hadn't used any birth control.

I'd been very lucky. I didn't think pregnancy would happen to *me*. I was too ashamed to tell my parents. I knew they'd be disappointed in me, and I was afraid of hurting and embarrassing them.

So Steve and I planned to set up an abortion. I knew there was a child—a life—inside me, but I wasn't thinking about the baby. I was concerned about my *own* life and the sacrifices a child would mean for my future.

I put off the abortion until three days before I was supposed to leave for college. When I got to the clinic, I realized I'd confused the dates and had waited so long I needed a two-day procedure. But I couldn't come back the next day, so I was really upset.

I sat in the waiting room for an hour, babbling and thinking stuff like, *What would my parents do if I told them?...It's not like they wouldn't love me anymore....If they found out I had an abortion, it would kill them.*

I finally stood and voiced my decision. "I can't do it!"

The counselor was ticked! She acted like I'd wasted her time and charged me $20 for counseling. What counseling? I'd watched a five-minute video.

ROUGH CONDITIONS AHEAD

Steve was mad when he learned Heather hadn't gone ahead with the abortion.

That was really the beginning of the end for us. I had to tell my parents because they expected me to leave for college. Mom was hysterical.

"How could you do this to me?" she said.

I quivered as Mom's face reddened in anger.

"You...you are *not* the girl I raised!"

Dad jumped in with an effort to calm things down. He said, "Heather, you made a mistake, but you're still our Heather!" That meant everything to me.

In time, her mother made the adjustment to Heather's pregnancy. Part of the problem was that Heather had shut her parents out since first discovering her pregnancy three months earlier.

After Mom accepted my situation, she really helped and supported me, and she even encouraged me to check out a local Christian college. I enrolled for the fall semester.

My mom also found out about a Christian adoption agency that provided shepherding homes—places where pregnant women can live until their babies are born. After I moved into one, Mom and I talked on the phone every night and grew very close by the end of my pregnancy.

The next few months were probably the loneliest in Heather's life. Her dad took her out for breakfast frequently, but she avoided seeing old friends or making new ones at college. And Steve? He had stopped coming around completely.

But God was close. He never walked away or left me hanging by myself. The more I deepened my relationship with Christ, the more He opened my eyes and helped me see things I should have noticed a long time ago. I discovered that Steve treated me unfairly and how unhealthy our relationship had been.

I sought God's help and asked for forgiveness. I was truly repentant—sorry not just for how I'd messed up my life, but for letting God down as well.

There was such a dramatic change in my relationship with Christ that I didn't feel like the same person! In one sense, I was really lonely because I was still too embarrassed to let even Molly see me. But I was spending a lot of time in God's company, reading and praying.

CROSSROADS

Heather had to make a decision: Keep the baby or give it up for adoption. She realized she'd have to sacrifice her dreams of school in order to support the two of them.

I wanted my baby to have a mother who would stay home to care for it. I also wanted it to have a mother *and a* father.

I needed to know what my parents thought, even though the decision was ultimately mine. Mom wouldn't give me a straight answer. I think she wanted to keep the baby in her family. But in her heart she knew it wasn't the best thing.

Finally, Dad said, "I want you to know that whatever you decide, I'll support you. But I *do* feel adoption is the right decision. I know you're thinking of your baby, but I'm considering *my* baby. Are you really ready to be a mother yet?" Dad's honesty helped me a lot.

I started planning an adoption. I prayed, "God, if I'm not supposed to do this, you've got to tell me." I didn't get any sky-script. I just felt adoption was the right choice because when I'd start questioning, He'd overwhelm me with a deep peace.

Heather began looking at profiles of people who wanted to adopt a baby. She kept coming back to David and Ann, a couple who had been married for 10 years. The way they wrote about their love for each other and for God—and how they wanted to share that love with a child—appealed to Heather.

My whole family went with me to meet them. I was tense. David, however, was laid-back, relaxed and did most of the talking. Ann was quiet, pretty. They asked me how *I* wanted the baby raised. I could tell they truly cared about *me*, not just my baby. By the end of the interview, I was convinced they were the right parents for my baby. They were ecstatic!

THE FINAL STRETCH

Heather describes her time in the hospital as "weird." Her labor was long and hard, and the drugs took time to wear off. The nurses kept coming and taking the baby—a little boy—and  *there were too many people in her room. To top things off, Steve came to see her, saying he planned to keep the baby.*

It was the first time he'd faced the idea of being a father. I yelled at him, "This is a life—not a toy to be fooled around with." Mom talked to him, and he finally changed his mind.

That afternoon Dad brought his Bible and read me the story of Abraham being asked by God to sacrifice his son Isaac because I felt that was what I was being asked to do, too.

After having spent no more than 20 minutes with Isaac, Heather left the hospital the next day.

My sister had to lay him in his crib—I couldn't do it. Dad went ahead of us to the car so we couldn't see him cry.

I don't remember anything except lying on the couch with my head in my mother's lap. I wept for two whole days. I didn't know it was possible to cry that hard.

I asked to meet David and Ann at the agency the day they were to take custody of Isaac. I held him for a moment. *How many lives,* I thought, *have been changed forever because I let down my guard?* I hurt so bad I thought I'd explode.

With tears streaming down my cheeks, I carried my son to his new parents. Ann didn't hesitate to grab him, and that's what I needed to see—that she felt he was *her* baby. Pictures were taken of the four of us together, and then I left.

Heather joined a birth mother's support group and organized her entire schedule around its meetings. She still longs to hold her baby at times, so much so that her arms ache. But she's healing. Heather is now married and a full-time, stay-at-home mom to her one-year-old son. She and her husband are both active in their local church.

I know *now* that Christian girls *can* compromise. They're not always strong. Some have even opted for abortion instead of adoption. But I also know what God can do. He loves us just as we are. No strings attached. I can't imagine getting through it without Him.

Kay Paulson is a free-lance writer from Littleton, Colo.

HOW TO HELP A PREGNANT FRIEND

Your friend thinks she's pregnant and has confided in you. Here are some suggestions on how to help her.

Don't be a "Lone Ranger." Another life is a big responsibility. Don't try to be your friend's only source of support. Express concern for her and then tell her you'd like to go with her to seek help.

Talk with adults. You may have a terrific group of friends, but they're not the people with whom to share her secret. Encourage her to talk with an *adult.* Whom should she confide in?

1. Her parents need to know. They'll probably find out sooner or later anyway, so try to convince her to share this secret with them—even if she's certain they'll flip.

2. A pastor, youth minister or Christian counselor is also a good choice. Help your friend understand that this is too big of a problem to handle by herself.

Get her to see a doctor. Home pregnancy tests are not always reliable, and there could be complications that your friend isn't even aware of. Try to help her see the importance of seeking medical help. But, again, her parents need to be in on this decision.

Keep reminding her that a life is a life is a life is a life! If she starts talking about the possibility of abortion, help her see that *thousands* of couples around the nation are waiting in line to adopt a baby. Beg her to give this little person a chance.

Be a friend. She already feels the magnitude of her dilemma. So don't add to the problem by condemning her. Continue to love her, listen to her heart, wipe her tears and help her sort through her thoughts. Pray *with* her and *for* her.

Hey Greg:

I found out at school last week that a girl I grew up with was raped by a guy from another school. They were just out on a date and he raped her! I can't believe it. I feel like getting some buddies and hurting the guy—bad! He just got bailed out of jail. I've heard he'll probably get away with it; that he'll say she wanted it. Why are some guys such jerks? —Missoula, Mont.

GREG: When I hear stuff like that I just want to throw up. Unfortunately, some guys have learned from *Playboy,* MTV, rap stars—or perhaps their dads—that girls want it even when they say no. That is literally NEVER the case. Respecting a girl's body isn't something that's talked about much—but it needs to be.

I want Susie to talk to girls about how they can protect themselves from guys who only have one thing on their minds.

Susie: Try to plan ahead. Don't wait till you need a way out to look for one! For example, always know where you're going and when you'll be back. A guy who says, "We'll just play it by ear" is a guy who probably wants to see how far he can get with you.

You're always better off dating someone you KNOW instead of someone you've just met. By agreeing to go out with a guy you don't know very well, you're taking some obvious risks. The exception? A blind date who comes highly endorsed from someone you respect a lot.

A few clues that could signal possible danger are someone who wants total control over you, an extremely jealous and possessive guy, or someone who talks openly about nasty sexual encounters.

(If you'd like more information on date rape, order the pamphlet "Date Rape" from Focus on the Family. Call 1-800-232-2649 and ask for item LF203.)

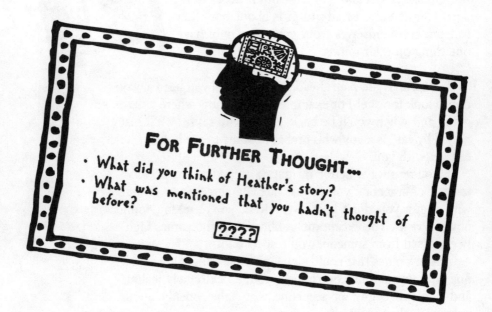

FOR FURTHER THOUGHT...

- What did you think of Heather's story?
- What was mentioned that you hadn't thought of before?

????

Now, a Few Words from Our Savior

We've mentioned this fact over and over: God has put His stamp of approval on sex—just keep it where it belongs; don't jump the gun. But what *specifically* does He say?

We believe the Bible to be the ultimate source of truth. Jesus said, "Then you will know the truth, and the truth will set you free" (John 8:32). But just how *do* His words set you free?

Once you know what's right, you can start *doing* right. Though no one says this much anymore, right has rewards and wrong has consequences. True freedom occurs when your conscience is clear, your standards are set in stone, and your actions don't betray your words. This is NOT an impossible goal to shoot for, either. If it was, God wouldn't challenge you to be up to the task—and neither would we!

Here is God's Word—His original intentions for sex:

"A man will leave his father and mother and be united to his wife, and they will become one flesh" (Gen. 2:24).

This verse is talking about marriage. Note that it doesn't say the man will leave his home and become united with whoever looks good.

"For out of the heart come evil thoughts, murder, adultery, sexual immorality, theft, false testimony, slander" (Matt. 15:19).

Jesus knows us better than we know ourselves, and these words tell us that the potential for sexual immorality is within all of us. That's why God didn't just send His Son to pay the penalty for our sin. He came to dwell within us, to give us the Power Source to tap into in order to withstand our natural tendency to sin.

It wasn't just our individual mistakes Jesus came to die for; it was our sinful nature that's constantly trying to convince us to betray what we really want (read Rom. 7:14—8:2).

"You shall not commit adultery" (Exod. 20:14).

This commandment means having sex with anyone other than your mate is not God's plan or ideal. Why? Sex is too special of a gift to give away to someone you won't be committed to for your entire life. It's such an intimate act. God knows—and many couples have learned—that the emotional consequences are devastating when a spouse cheats.

"Marriage should be honored by all, and the marriage bed kept pure, for God will judge the adulterer and all the sexually immoral" (Heb. 13:4).

What kind of judgment is God referring to? This verse isn't talking about sending anyone who has ever made a mistake to hell. Sometimes, however, there are natural consequences (a disease), or perhaps consequences in marriage similar to the difficult sexual adjustments Greg talked about in chapter 1.

"The acts of the sinful nature are obvious: sexual immorality, impurity and debauchery;...I warn you, as I did before, that those who live like this will not inherit the kingdom of God" (Gal. 5:19,21).

This verse is a little more specific about the spiritual consequences for those "who live like this." Another version says, "Those who *practice* such things will not inherit the kingdom of God" (NKJV). Again, the verse is not talking about a few mistakes that occur in youth; it's talking about a consistent lifestyle of obeying the sinful nature.

"The body is not meant for sexual immorality, but for the Lord, and the Lord for the body....Flee from sexual immorality. All other sins a man commits are outside his body, but he who sins sexually sins against his own body" (1 Cor. 6:13,18).

Our lives weren't paid for by the blood of Jesus Christ so we can indulge in whatever we want. Our lives were paid for so that we could be used by God to bring glory to Him. If you're a Christian, God wants to use your body. If you give it over to accomplish your own purposes, God can't use you as He wants. It's that simple.

"But among you there must not be even a hint of sexual immorality, or of any kind of impurity, or of greed, because these are improper for God's holy people" (Eph. 5:3).

We know what happens to pastors and church leaders who make a sexual mistake, but what happens to the rest of us? If there is a true rumor going around about what you did sexually, how will that affect your witness to the One who died for you? Often (though not always), it completely destroys a person's Christian witness. Consequently, the years that could have been your most productive as a Christian (helping people choose Jesus and heaven) could be utterly disqualified because you didn't race according to the rules.

"But a man who commits adultery lacks judgment; whoever does so destroys himself" (Prov. 6:32).

Ask any Christian man or woman the consequences of

committing adultery, and many would quote this verse word for word. It IS potentially destroying to a reputation, a career, a happy marriage, the children—everything that was right can suddenly turn wrong by making a poor choice and committing adultery.

"Put to death, therefore, whatever belongs to your earthly nature: sexual immorality, impurity, lust, evil desires and greed, which is idolatry" (Col. 3:5).

The only way to bury a human trait that keeps coming to the surface is to daily—sometimes hourly—call on God's power and God's protection. Because sexual influences are so pervasive, relying on our own willpower to overcome sexual temptation is practically a lost cause.

Does God call us to live holy lives so He can watch us struggle with the impossible? No! When God called us to holiness, He also gave us everything we need to live as He wants us to. There's absolutely no way in your own strength you can be all that God wants you to be without giving His Holy Spirit free reign to work in your life. The answer is to GIVE UP! Tell Him you're tired of trying and surrender EVERYTHING to His Lordship. Ask Him to give you the Holy Spirit's power so you *can* lead a holy life.

If you're struggling in this area *(not EVERY teen will have a problem)*, you also need to enlist the prayer support of those who know you best: Ask your dad (if you're a guy) or your mom (if you're a girl) to pray for you each day. Make a pact with a couple of your best Christian friends to pray for each other every day. Tell your youth leader to pray specifically for you. Better yet, have him ask people in your church to "adopt a teen in prayer." Among the other things about which they can pray for you, they can ask that God would keep you away from temptation and sexual immorality.

Sex is a major spiritual battle, and it cannot be fought without spiritual weapons (see Eph. 6:10-18).

"Having lost all sensitivity, they have given themselves over to sensuality so as to indulge in every kind of impurity, with a continual lust for more" (Eph. 4:19).

By continually allowing your mind to dwell on sex, allowing your eyes to view sexual acts, or allowing your body to practice sexual immorality, you will lose a sensitivity to its destructive power. That is, you'll begin to think there's nothing wrong with it, and you'll get mad or not listen to those who attempt to point you back to the truth. When this happens, God stands back and lets you choose your own course. He will not control your will. As we've said before, He loves you too much to make you a puppet. When God gives you over to your sensuality, you're out from under His protection. The consequences you incur will therefore be caused by you.

"For everything in the world—the cravings of sinful man, the lust of his eyes and the boasting of what he has and does—comes not from the Father but from the world" (1 John 2:16).

God has given us the desire for sexual intimacy, but the world (Satan) tries to move us to the next level—craving. Many teens admit they have gone past the normal desire for the opposite sex to an "uncontrollable" craving for sexual release. In essence, they're addicted.

You CAN become addicted to sex. Pornography, movies, masturbation (which we'll talk about next), even a lust for someone of the same sex can be addicting. Though everyone hates to admit they are actually controlled by something like sex, our world—your city—is full of people who are addicted to sex. Through constant exposure and an out-of-control thought-life, sex can be overwhelming. When this occurs, we recommend professional help.

If sexual addiction doesn't actually kill someone, it will give them so much guilt and anguish they will wind up hating themselves for what they've become.

WHAT ABOUT THAT PERPLEXING HABIT?

At *Breakaway,* I'll (Greg) get frequent anonymous letters from guys who want to know what God thinks about masturbation—solo sexual gratification. Some guys admit being controlled by this perplexing habit. The guilt they feel is intolerable.

"Does God hate me?"

"Am I a pervert?"

"Will I ever overcome it?"

I wasn't a Christian in high school, and sadly, at an early age I was exposed to pornography. As I went through my teen years, it was always accessible (my dad even brought it home!). You can't look at that stuff and not want to masturbate. Though it's embarrassing to admit, especially in a book like this for all the world to see, I had a big problem with it. Except, because I wasn't a Christian, I didn't feel particularly guilty. I learned from other guys (who were also non-Christians) that it was "normal."

After I became a Christian at age 18, my four-year habit didn't automatically disappear. Though marriage at age 20 and a growing faith put that desire on hold, the habit came back a few years later. It's a MAJOR bum feeling to be doing something solo that could be fulfilled with your spouse.

Guys, here is a true statement: *The habits we learn early in life are the toughest to break.*

It's an awful feeling to be enslaved by something so stupid as masturbation. Though age, the Lord and accountability to other men (which has been the best decision I could ever make) have allowed me to keep this habit under control for many years, those thoughts—and a desire to be visually stimulated—are still a constant battle. This habit, learned early, has caused me more grief and guilt than any other.

Guys, no, *men,* you MUST work on conquering this habit—NOW! Only *you* can choose to go against the tide and allow your eyes and mind to be controlled by the Spirit. If you don't do it now, other spirits are more than able to fill the void that God's Spirit could have filled.

What does the Bible say about masturbation?

It never mentions the word. Perplexing, right? Does that mean God doesn't care about it? Or does it mean it's so obviously wrong God didn't sense a need to mention it by name? I wish I knew.

First, I urge you that, if you have a father at home, you talk to him about it (girls, talk to your mothers). We wouldn't want to say anything different from the message they give you. Sure, it will be uncomfortable, but please don't worry about that. Too much is at stake to live in silence.

Second, search the Scriptures. Along with the ones mentioned on the previous pages that may apply, here are a few we have found that seem to relate.

"You were bought at a price. Therefore honor God with your body" (1 Cor. 6:20).

"For God did not call us to be impure, but to live a holy life" (1 Thess. 4:7).

"For you have spent enough time in the past doing what pagans choose to do—living in debauchery, lust, drunkenness, orgies, carousing and detestable idolatry" (1 Pet. 4:3).

"So I say, live by the Spirit, and you will not gratify the desires of the sinful nature. For the sinful nature desires what is contrary to the Spirit, and the Spirit what is contrary to the sinful nature. They are in conflict with each other, so that you do not do what you want" (Gal. 5:16,17).

Though the percentage of females who masturbate is far less than males, we know that it can still cause a tremendous amount of guilt among girls (as well as guys).

Here are the facts: Masturbation is NOT the unpardonable sin. Though it is frustrating, stupid and a habit tough to break, if you feel guilt because of it, God does forgive—EVERY TIME YOU ASK.

Does that mean if I do it every day, truly knowing that for me it's wrong, and ask God to forgive me, He'll do it?

That's exactly what it means! If it doesn't, a lot of Christian teens—and adults—are in big trouble!

Tim Stafford, who writes the column "Love, Sex, and the Whole Person" in *Campus Life* magazine wrote the following:

Paul offers a very personal statement about a thorn in the flesh in 2 Corinthians 12:7-9 that may shed light on why, when teens pray that God would remove this from them, God seems silent. There, Paul, talking about how he could very easily be a proud person, says, "To keep me from being too elated...a thorn was given me in the flesh, a messenger of Satan, to harass me,...Three times I besought the Lord about this, that it should leave me; but he said to me, 'My grace is sufficient for you, for my power is made perfect in weakness'" (*RSV*).

I don't suppose Paul is speaking of masturbation there, but what he says might apply. Anyone living under the drive to masturbate knows what it means to feel weak and foolish. Why doesn't God take the urge away? Perhaps for the very reason that He didn't take Paul's thorn away: to remind us that we are not saved on our personal purity, nor by our knowledge of the Bible, but by God's loving grace, which comes to us no matter how bad or weak we are. We are good enough for God, just as we are. Perhaps that "thorn-in-the-flesh" urge that is so difficult to control can be a reminder of how much we need Him, constantly.

FOR FURTHER THOUGHT...

- What was the most sobering thing your read in this chapter?
- What was the most encouraging thing you read in this chapter?
- What in your life is a reminder to you that you need God constantly?

????

How Far Is Too Far?

We know what some of you are thinking, *OK, I realize the Bible tells us not to have sex before we're married, but it doesn't say anything about...you know...all the other stuff.* And you're right, it doesn't.

Hey, how'd you know that's what I was thinking?

Cuz we're writing the book, and we remember what it was like when we were teens.

Hmmm. So if I wrote a book, I'D know all the stuff that the readers are thinking?

Don't press it. Back to the subject—

Sex.

Didn't take you long to get back on track, did it?

I'm a teen, remember? I think about sex once in a while.

OK, OK. You're right. The Bible comes out clear and strong on premarital sex, but it says nothing about petting and getting *close* to having sex.

Why is that?

I think it's because back in Bible times there was no such thing as dating. When you reached age 15 (or so), your parents picked out a mate for you, and you got married.

Ugh!

But the *good* side was, teens didn't have to go through as much sexual temptation as you do. About the time their hormones woke up and went wacko, they got married and didn't have to worry about it anymore.

That would be a relief!

But just because the Bible doesn't mention petting doesn't mean it's a wise thing to do.

I don't know. I believe...I mean, I have FRIENDS who believe that you can do anything you want, and if you don't actually have intercourse, you're OK.

You're OK? Meaning what? You're OK in God's sight? Or you're OK because you won't get pregnant?

Well...both, I guess.

Well, if you don't have sexual intercourse you can't get pregnant, but that certainly doesn't mean everything else is permissible in God's sight.

Why not? Sexual intercourse is sexual intercourse. Anything else oughta be all right!

What does sexual intercourse do? Besides being created to be a pleasurable experience, God invented it to bond two people closer than they've ever been before. It *cements* a relationship. But *any* sexual activity (even hand-holding and kissing) acts like a glue and begins bonding two people.

So?

So sexual intercourse isn't the only way to have an orgasm. If you or your partner are brought to sexual climax (through mutual masturbation), you've created the same result that sexual intercourse would bring. And guess what? In *God's* eyes, it's sexual sin.

Yikes!

You see, intercourse isn't the only thing you can do to "go too far." Part of establishing GODLY dating relationships means not doing *anything* you'll regret later.

I see what you're saying. But sometimes it's just reallyreallyreally hard to stop.

That may be because you've started climbing too fast on a ladder of natural progression.

What in the WORLD are you talking about?

There's a natural, built-in progression to ALL relationships. If you stop and *think* about each level, you can stop yourself from going too far.

What IS this progression thing?

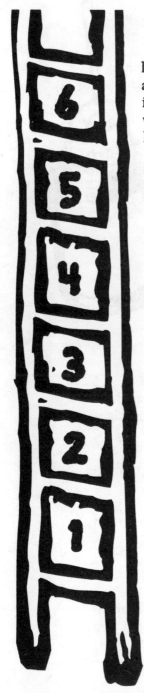

It's kind of like a ladder.[1] Let's set it up like this:

1. Looking at someone's body. You can learn a lot about someone from that first glance—sex, approximate age, height, weight. If you place a lot of importance on outward appearance, this first glance will tell you if you're attracted to the person you're looking at.

2. Making eye contact. It's kind of embarrassing to have a member of the opposite sex catch you looking at him/her, isn't it? When your eyes meet, the natural thing is to look away. It's a moment that can be uncomfortable. When you start to like each other, though, you become comfortable maintaining eye contact for short periods of time. You'll probably also smile, which is a good sign that each of you is interested in the other.

3. Talking with someone of the opposite sex. Your first chats are usually just surface stuff. You ask things such as, "What's your name?" "What school do you go to?" "How'd you do on Mrs. Stevens history test?" "What church do you attend?" This is a friendship stage. You're getting to know each other. If you continue to like each other, your friendship will deepen.

4. Holding hands. This is a sign of attachment. You like each other. You're becoming more than friends. Your relationship is growing.

5. Hands on shoulders. This stage of friendship includes hugging. Yes, you sometimes hug your buddies, but probably by now, you're thinking of this person as much more than a buddy. In fact, you're thinking of him/her a *lot!* When you *do* hug, it's a warm, affectionate embrace. Though it's not real love, this stage of your relationship begins to signal your feelings for each other.

6. Hands on waist. By this time your friendship has definitely become a romantic relationship. You may even be calling yourselves boyfriend/girlfriend. You might be walking with your arms around one another's waist. By this stage, you're probably sharing secrets with each other.

7. Kissing on the cheek. Becoming closer makes you more comfortable with the face-to-face stage. You enjoy looking into one another's eyes and have learned definite signals (a wink, half-grin, etc.) that enable you to communicate at times without words.

8. Kissing on the lips. At this stage, sexual desire is awakened and becomes a definite factor in your relationship. You're experiencing a bonding that is sexually stimulating. You may also be using your hands to stroke his/her cheeks or hair while kissing and talking. You feel emotionally close. French kissing (your tongue inside his/her mouth) can also occur during this stage.

(**The final four.** The remaining levels of our progressive ladder should be considered very private and reserved for marriage.)

9. Petting over or under clothes. If you're experimenting with this stage, you're playing with fire and will probably move to the next stage without even thinking about it.

10. Petting with clothes removed. Again, this should be reserved for marriage. You're sharing the intimate parts of your body with someone who is *not* your marriage partner. In God's eyes, this is wrong.

11. External genital contact and orgasm. You're actually stealing from your future husband/wife. If you're involved in this stage, please seek adult counsel and consider the possibility of ending the relationship. *Why?* Because God is definitely not pleased with your physical activity.

12. Sexual intercourse. You've given away the most important and special gift you can ever present to your future mate.

Can you see how getting too physical really begins *waaay* before intercourse? It's not just the complete sex act that God is concerned with—He's concerned about *all* physical contact.

There are degrees of sexual fulfillment in the final stages right *before* actual intercourse. And for you to be sexually fulfilled by someone other than your husband/wife is *wrong* in God's eyes.

Wow. I get it now.

Do you understand the importance of going slowly and maintaining your ground on the first few steps?

Yeah. It all makes sense. But how do I know which step is too far for me? I mean, maybe a kiss is wrong for some people.

Great question. And I'd like to answer that by giving *you* some questions. Seek God's guidance and strive to answer the following questions with *absolute honesty*. Ask each question about each level of the ladder. When you answer yes, determine to make that your limit.

☑ SEX CHECK:

☐ Does my conscience bother me? Do I feel any guilt at all about what I've done?

☐ Does doing what I've done make me want to go all the way? Am I lusting instead of loving?

☐ Do I feel manipulated, obligated or pressured to do this?

☐ Can I be honest with my parents about what I've done?

☐ Would my parents approve of what I've done?

☐ Am I still seeing this person through God's eyes? Am I caring and respecting him/her as God wants me to?

☐ Could this have negative consequences?

☐ When I'm with my husband/wife someday, will I look back on this and regret that I've done it?

☐ Am I being sexually fulfilled by this?

If you have trouble answering any of these questions in relation to where you are on the progressive ladder, seek the advice of your parents, youth leader or pastor.

Dear Susie:

Why do girls get bad names after having sex, but the guys become "men" and other guys look up to them? — **Bonne Terre, Mo.**

Susie: That's a good question. Greg, will you answer it?

GREG: It's called a "double standard." Let me explain.

In previous decades, girls who were sexually active were called "easy" or "sluts." There was still an expectation in society that it was the role of females to stay virgins until marriage. MTV, Madonna, Janet Jackson, the feminist movement and other influences have helped changed that attitude—somewhat. In many high schools, however, a girl who sleeps around with tons of guys can still get a bad reputation, and the girl who is waiting is still held in high regard.

Among non-Christian guys, losing your virginity is like a rite of passage (something that has to happen before you're a man). It's been that way for generations. Movies and TV do very little to contradict this destructive thought—most reinforce it. Consequently, we have two different standards: guys can do it, girls shouldn't. That double standard, though, has likely saved a lot of girls the heartache of giving themselves away before marriage. One good standard is better than none!

FOR FURTHER THOUGHT...

- You may have realized that you've gone too far on the ladder of progression. What will you do now?
- How can prolonged kissing get you in trouble?
- Have you taken the time to talk with God about establishing your stopping point (or limit) on the ladder of progression?
- Why is it important to know where your stopping point is? What could happen if you're unsure?

????

Note

1. The progressive ladder of sexuality was inspired by Donald M. Joy's, *Becoming a Man* (Ventura, CA: Regal Books, 1990), chaps. 5,6.

PART V

Tough Issues

Sexually Transmitted Diseases
Pornography
Abortion
Homosexuality
Divorce-Proofing Your Life

How Safe IS Sex?

Seven years ago, Tina Brown was the average all-American girl. She was pretty, smart, athletic and popular. As a *sophomore*, she was getting calls from *senior* guys for dates nearly every weekend. At first, she held her ground when the guys wanted to do more than make out. But she was a new Christian and still had a long way to go before her faith was really grounded. It wasn't long before one of her dates pressured her into having sex. He was a guy who'd had dozens of girls before Tina. After a few more weekends, he dumped her.

Tina felt bad, but instead of learning from her mistake, she thought that since she'd blown it, there was no reason to try to stay pure. She had five more boyfriends—all upperclassmen—her sophomore year. Each one included sex in the weekend ritual.

She had heard all about sexually transmitted diseases (STDs) in health class, and she always made sure the guy wore a condom.

At the beginning of her junior year, she rededicated

her life to the Lord. She wanted to change, and change she did. She was a whole new person! But in a routine physical she told her doctor about some sores she had around her mouth. He ran a test and discovered she had herpes-1.

Today, she's still committed to the Lord, still young and attractive—but she will carry this STD with her the rest of her life. Her future husband will have to know before they marry, and there's a strong possibility any children she bears will be born with the disease.

Tina thought she knew all about STDs. She thought she had taken the proper precautions. She was wrong.

Are you tired of hearing about AIDS and condoms and safe sex and STDs yet? We talk to teens all the time who say they've heard it all, and they're tired of it. If you think you know all the facts on stuff like this, skip to the next chapter; we don't want to bore or offend you.

But what "facts" have you heard?

WHAT THE FUTURE HOLDS

Tina caught herpes in the 1980s. Even with all of the information available these days, it won't just be herpes that Christian teens will be infected with in the '90s. They'll become HIV positive. Let's admit this fact: Teens at your school WILL NOT die of AIDS during their high school years. But at your 10-year reunion, several classmates and friends *will* have died from unknowingly contracting the AIDS virus during their high school years.

We don't say this to scare you. It's simply a fact. Count on it! Young men and women who have their whole lives ahead of them will have it snuffed out in their prime because they believed everything their health class taught them about condoms and safe sex. Instead of waiting for the one to share themselves with in marriage, they "experimented." For some, all it will take is one sexual encounter with the wrong person to contract HIV, the virus that's a guaranteed killer.

It's the mid-'90s and AIDS is no longer a male homosexual disease. By the year 2000, heterosexuals will be contracting it at nearly the same rate as homosexuals do now. Will science find a cure? There's been an all-out war against cancer since 1960. Our government has spent billions and billions of dollars on research. No cure is in sight.

Here are the real facts about AIDS:

• You can't get the HIV virus from kissing—even deep kissing. It's spread through the blood, semen and vaginal fluids. (This disqualifies toilet seats in case you were wondering. When HIV is exposed to the air—like sperm—it dies.)

• There IS a chance of becoming HIV positive even if you wear a condom. Because condoms are made out of latex, they can have microscopic holes in them. The smallest detectable hole in a condom is one micron. The HIV virus is one-tenth the size of that hole!

• Do condoms prevent pregnancy? In 1989, Planned Parenthood, the leading abortion provider in the nation, admitted that condoms failed to prevent *pregnancy* 15.7 percent of the time over the course of the year. For girls under age 18, the failure rate was 18.4 percent. The HIV virus is 450 times smaller than the sperm that escapes through a condom!

At a World Congress for 800 sexologists in Heidelberg, Germany, these experts were asked if *they* would trust a condom for their own protection against AIDS. Not one of the 800 raised their hands.

So why does the government push the "miracle of condoms" down the throats of public school teens when it's aware of these facts? Even though they know that condoms break, leak and teens think they, themselves, are invincible so they rarely use condoms, why are they suddenly the end-all in preventing the spread of HIV?

The reason: The government has given up. They're convinced that because teens have no ability to keep their clothes on, someone better do *something* so teenagers don't *all* become HIV positive.

Some condom distribution opponents believe that handing out condoms to teens will simply encourage more sexual activity among them. We believe it does, too. But even if it doesn't, what the government seems to be doing is handing teens a gun and saying, "Be careful. There's one bullet left in the chamber. But chances are when you pull the trigger, you won't get hurt." Thanks a lot, gov.

The Point

We could take a few thousand more words and talk about other STDs such as chlamydia, gonorrhea, pelvic inflammatory disease (PID), genital warts and syphilis (3 million new cases of STDs are being reported each year). But we're not going to do this because even most school health textbooks can explain the truth about these.

The point isn't to bombard you with statistics, percentages and a bunch of facts you're going to forget by tomorrow. Yes, we do feel a need to fire a warning shot by telling you the truth about a few things, but we know that even this likely won't work if you find yourself in a compromising position.

What we do want is to appeal to those who are toying with the idea of risking their lives for a few moments of sexual pleasure. Susie has never been married and is still a virgin. I've been married for years. We both agree on this fact: Although sex is a wonderful part of marriage, 10 seconds of intense pleasure is not worth dying for!

Although this chapter has talked about a few physical dangers of premarital sexual activity, we don't believe these are the strongest arguments for remaining sexually abstinent. The ONE who created us, the ONE who died for us—He has said a few things about the subject, too.

FOR FURTHER THOUGHT...

· Do teens consider getting an STD when they choose to experiment sexually? Do you? Why or why not?
· Do you think all the government education has helped teens make better decisions? Why has it been or not been effective?
· What do you think you and your friends need to know about STDs? What would be the best source of information? Who would you listen to?

????

"I've Already Blown It! NOW What?"

A couple of years ago I (Susie) received a letter from a 16-year-old girl saying she was pregnant. Her story went like this:

> I'm a Christian and am very involved in my church. I always planned on waiting until marriage to have sex, but got in with the wrong crowd and started doing some things I knew were wrong—like drinking.
>
> One of my girlfriends had a party, and even though I KNEW there would be alcohol, I went anyway. Everyone started drinking, including me. I only had a little. I wasn't drunk, but I knew I was in the wrong place at the wrong time.
>
> My girlfriend's dad came to the house, drunk, and started flirting with me. We went upstairs—I thought just to talk—but he forced himself on me.
>
> I told my girlfriend and she disowned me. I guess she thinks I came on to him or something. Up to this point, I was sexually inactive. He stole my virginity.

I felt used and worthless. Since my non-Christian boyfriend had been pressuring me to have sex with him, and since I was no longer a virgin, I went ahead and gave in. I figured, "Why not? I'm already used, so I might as well go ahead and do it all the time. No sense waiting anymore."

My boyfriend and I had sex only a few times when I found out I was pregnant. He dropped me like a hot potato. Please pray for me. I believe abortion is wrong, and I don't want to do more wrong on top of what I've already done, so I've decided to have the baby. I know I have a tough road ahead of me. Will you pray for me?

I had never met Jackie, but I *did* begin praying for her. Later, I decided to look up her number and try to reach her by phone, as she lived in a nearby city in Colorado. Her dad answered and told me she was in a Colorado Springs hospital with pregnancy complications. I asked his permission to visit.

I phoned Jackie and asked if I could pick up anything for her before coming by. We chatted for a few minutes, and she dropped some hints about a favorite ice cream treat. After stopping at Dairy Queen to pick up a Butterfinger Blizzard, I opened the door to her room.

We made small talk. She ate the ice cream. Finally, I asked if I could confront her with some tough questions.

"Jackie, when would you say your mistakes began?"

"Probably about two years ago. I was home-schooled all my life until two years ago. I went to a private Christian school and just got mixed up with the wrong crowd. I should have looked for friends who believed like my family and me—you know, kids who had values.

"We've always gone to church," she continued. "And my entire family is *very* involved. I'm active in our youth group, go to Bible study and really love the Lord.

"But I was suddenly faced with a group of kids who were doing a bunch of things I'd never experienced before. They bragged about their weekend parties, and I couldn't help but wonder what it was like.

"Then when they started including me, I felt special—you know, like I belonged. So I started hanging out with them. I guess that's when the trouble started."

She took a few more scoops of her Blizzard, and I asked, "Have you asked God for forgiveness?"

"Yes, and I know He's forgiven me. I'm in the process now of straightening out my life and trying to regain some lost ground. My mom is home-schooling me again, and I think I'll be able to finish high school early. Of course—" she paused. "I may not be able to do all the things I'd hoped."

"What were your dreams?" I asked.

"To go to college. Study music. Do something for God."

"You can still go to college," I reminded her.

"Yeah, I know. And I will. It'll just be different, that's all. I'll have to spread it out instead of getting through in four straight years. I have a baby to care for now. That changes *everything*."

"Are your parents supportive?" I asked.

"They've been great!" Jackie responded. "Mom and Dad are committed to helping me with the baby. They want me to go to college and try to fulfill as many of my dreams as I can. And even though I'm excited about God's forgiveness and giving birth, I still go back in my mind sometimes and play it over and over and over again. What if I *hadn't* gotten mixed up with the wrong crowd? What if I *hadn't* let down my guard?"

"Jackie, suppose there are some teen girls who are considering letting down their guard. Maybe their boyfriends are pressuring them or they're just curious about sex and want to give in. What advice would you give them?"

"The movies and TV really build it up. It's supposed to be some huge, romantic, wonderful experience that you'll cherish the rest of your life. You know what really happens?" she said. "It's over in five minutes! The movies lie. So does TV. When teens are having sex, it's usually not in the most romantic place imaginable. And there's always the fear of getting caught—maybe you're in his house and his parents are gone—but you keep wondering if someone's going to come in unexpectedly. It's *not* a relaxing situation.

"So," she continued. "I'd tell girls that five minutes is certainly *not* worth giving up the best gift I could have given my future husband.

"You know what else I'd tell them?" she asked.

"What's that?"

"I'd tell them that I often wonder what it would have been like if I'd waited. You know, on my honeymoon with the man I'm committed to spending the rest of my life with. It *could* have been romantic, and special and meaningful. But I've missed that. Yes, I'm forgiven, and the Lord may still bring a godly man into my life, but I'll always have to deal with the consequences of letting down my guard."

By this time the Blizzard was gone. I prayed with Jackie and left. As I drove out of the parking lot, I couldn't help feeling a wave of sadness sweep over me. Yes, she's on the right track *now*, but to what degree will she have to forfeit her dreams? There's another life at stake now. I knew it wouldn't be easy.

"Be extra close to her, Lord," I prayed. "Comfort her, strengthen her and help her to continue walking with You."

Maybe you, like Jackie, have already blown it. God is willing to forgive and forget. So what is *your* responsibility? To seek His forgiveness. *And* to start over—as in establishing some new dating standards.

Don't try to do this on your own. Ask your parents, your youth leader or a trusted adult friend to help. And, as you date, allow them to hold you accountable. Give them the freedom to ask you some very personal questions about your dating relationships—including what you wear, how you act, if you've allowed your date to kiss you or not.

Isaiah 43:19 says, "I'm going to do a brand new thing!" *(TLB)*. And that's exactly what He wants to do in *your* life. It's called a "second virginity." If you've had sex, you're no longer a virgin. But God wants to forgive and *forget*, remember? In other words, He wants to wipe your slate completely clean—as if you'd never blown it!

What a wonderful and powerful God, huh? So, through His forgiveness and cleansing, you can claim a "second virginity." In *His* eyes—because He's blotted out your past—you're starting all over, a *virgin!*

If you've blown it, will you take a second to seek His forgiveness right now? Or, if you have a *friend* who has been sexually active, will you suggest he/she talk to the Lord? Here's a suggested prayer:

Father, I realize You know me much better than I know myself. And I know now that when You created Your perfect plan of sex within marriage, You did it out of love and protection for me.

I've blown it, Lord. I gave in, and I shouldn't have. I took control of my own life and broke Your perfect plan. I wish I hadn't. I wish I could go back and undo what I've done. I'm really sorry. Will You forgive me? Will You help me start over?

Give me the courage to go to a Christian adult and ask for some accountability. I need help in reestablishing my dating standards.

Lord, I want to have GODLY dating relationships. Help me to see my date as Your creation—holy and not to be tampered with. Thank You for Your promise to help me begin again—fresh, clean, new. Thank You for forgiving me and for seeing me as a brand-new virgin.

Be my strength, Jesus. When I'm tempted, help me to rely on Your power, not my own. I love You, Father. THANK YOU!

Yes. You're clean. And as Jesus would say, "Go and sin no more" (John 8:11, *NKJV*).

FOR FURTHER THOUGHT...

- What was most striking about Jackie's story?
- What do these passages say about forgiveness?
  - Psalm 103:11-13
  - Luke 5:21
  - 1 John 1:9
- Is God serious when He talks about His desire to offer His forgiveness to you?
- Do you really believe it?
- What is accountability? Do you think it is important?
- Are you allowing yourself to be held accountable? If so, by whom? If not, who will you ask to hold you accountable in your dating?

????

What Girls Think About Guys Who Look at Porn

We've mentioned it a number of times so far in this book: pornography. Not everyone has been exposed to it, true. But teenage guys, unfortunately, seem to stumble onto it somehow. Perhaps accidentally they find it at a neighbor's, some guy's locker at school, the convenience store down the street. Did you know there are more stores selling pornographic magazines and videos than there are McDonald's restaurants?

While guys are busy being curious, what are girls thinking? They know guys are looking at this stuff. I asked eight girls some very honest questions. Here are their honest answers.

How do you feel, knowing some guys have *Playboy* centerfolds on their wall?
Liz: After a guy looks at a Playmate, it seems as if he's undressing you with his eyes.

Amy: It makes me feel so uncomfortable!

Lindsey: I instantly feel pressure. I feel humiliated and want to get away from that room and that guy.

Shari: These models are posed in all kinds of weird positions, ready and waiting. It's not a realistic picture of what a girl really wants to do.

Merritt: The thought of guys looking at pornography makes my stomach turn. It reduces me from a valuable person to nothing.

How do you think porn affects the guys you know?

Liz: When guys focus on pornography, they start treating us differently. They talk dirty and grab us in embarrassing places. I don't think they realize how much this hurts us.

Shelby: It's giving guys a superficial look at girls. They start treating us as objects for their obsessions. It's like they don't care what's inside us anymore.

Erin: If guys wouldn't look at porn, fewer rapes would happen. When they look at it all the time, sex is all they can think of, all they want. I believe they might end up doing anything they can to get it. That's how Ted Bundy said he started!

Merritt: There's a guy at our school who brags about the porno films and magazines he looks at. None of the girls can stand him. Everything that comes out of his mouth is macho-bragging sex stuff. But then last week I saw him crying because his grandma died. I cared about him all of a sudden. If he would stop being so influenced by the porno stuff, he'd probably be a real nice guy.

Liz: I wish the guys could know how much it turns us off when they talk about porn. We lose respect for them, and it actually scares us.

Shannon: I've got a message

to guys out there: We'll never have a good relationship if we can't treat each other with respect. You can't respect a girl once you start focusing on what's underneath her clothes!

How hard is it to find a guy who treats you as a whole person and not just a sex object?

Shannon: What a girl wants more than anything is a guy who bases a girl's value on who she is—her personality, faith and talents. Most guys seem only interested in a girl's looks and how much she'll put out.

Liz: The Christian guys get snatched up first, if they act like one. They seem to concentrate on friendship first, which is the most important thing in a relationship.

Lindsey: It's hard! I'd rather not date a guy with a dirty mind, even if he's cuter than a guy with good values. What I want more than anything is true love and respect.

Amy: When I'm with a guy who treats me like a sex object, I want to go home and take a shower. I want a guy with a clean mind. Are you out there somewhere?

Do you feel you have to compete with the images guys see?

Shari: I don't want to, but all the other girls are wearing miniskirts and are getting noticed for it.

Amy: Guys expect girls to have "*Playboy* bodies." I know we're constantly worried about whether we're fat. Maybe that's why anorexia is such a problem.

Liz: I admit I giggle when the guys make dirty comments, mostly because that's what all the other girls do. I think none of us wants to egg them on, but we don't know how else to react.

Erin: Most girls do wear two-piece bathing suits. It's kind of a compliment when guys like your body, but then it's an insult, too. It's very confusing. Maybe if we got attention more for our personality we wouldn't have to use our bodies to try and compete. We really don't want to.

Some guys are notorious for wanting it both ways. They want the physical pleasure now, but they also want a woman who is pure and still has her self-respect in marriage.

On the other hand, I've talked to guys who've said they wish they could go back and start over. They want to start treating girls with respect instead of believing the lies pornography wants to tell you.

Though guys think it's just a nasty little secret that no one knows about, they're wrong. These girls knew, and so do the girls at your school. So does God. He really wants your minds to be pure.

This article by Lisa Kragerud first appeared in the October 1990 issue of *Breakaway*. Lisa lives near Seattle.

FOR FURTHER THOUGHT...

- What are some other potential consequences for allowing pornography to fill your brain?
- Who benefits most from the porn industry?
- How can Satan use pornography to change a guy's focus?

????

"Is It Really a Baby?"

You're in health class and the subject is abortion. "What if you're raped?" Mary Beth asks. "Certainly *that* would be a situation in which *everyone* would agree that abortion would be the best option."

"Yeah, I'll buy that," Joey says.

"Or what if you know the baby's gonna be deformed?" Carla says. "I don't wanna give birth to a handicapped child. I should be able to abort if I want to."

"I agree," Nancy says. "It's a woman's body. She should be able to decide."

Seems like the whole class is in agreement that there are times when abortion is OK. What do *you* think? *Are* there times when God looks the other way? Or times our Creator says, "Yeah, go ahead. This one's not perfect."

Since you're of dating age now, you'll begin to think about abortion more than ever during the next few years. You'll also start thinking about birth control, pregnancy—and your future. So do you mind if we take a few minutes to think hard about abortion? Check out this true story.

WHEN LILACS BLOOMED

Are there SOME situations in which abortion is justified? A nurse tells HER side.
By Kathy Schriefer, R.N.

The early morning sun was already warming the earth on that lovely spring day in 1973. The city of Rochester, New York, was preparing for its annual Lilac Festival, and the scent of hundreds of fragrant bushes filled the air. Birds chorused as background to my own humming as I walked across the park to the hospital.

I bubbled with anticipation of the day: I was scheduled to observe a Caesarean birth, and I smiled at the thought. A junior-year nursing student, I was spending my first week on a hospital maternity floor. Although I had already witnessed several births that week, the privilege of being present as a newborn drew its first breath left me amazed and hungry for more.

Leaving the beauty of nature, I pushed open the door to the hospital lobby. Here the sights, sounds and smells were different. The strong odor of antiseptic cleansers stung my nostrils. Highly waxed floor tiles beamed brightly. A voice blared from a loudspeaker, paging a doctor.

I was reminded that I was entering a battlefield, a place where a fierce fight against death and disease was waged daily. Nowhere else, it seemed to me, was the essence of life such a sacred trust. I felt proud to be a part of such a noble undertaking.

In the elevator, I stared down at my newly polished white nursing shoes and took deep, slow breaths to calm my fluttery stomach. When the doors finally slid open, I quickly checked in with my instructor and headed for the dressing area. I didn't want to miss one moment of this exciting experience.

In the dressing room I stuffed my uniform into a locker and threw on a green cotton scrub dress. Drawing another deep breath, I hurried to the scrub room. There I awkwardly tucked my hair into a paper cap and thoroughly washed my hands. Just as I was reaching for a sterile gown to cover my scrub dress, the head nurse entered the room and explained that there'd been a change: The Caesarean delivery had been canceled. I tried hard not to let her see my disappointment, but my shoulders sagged slightly.

"I'm sure you're disappointed," she observed and then, brightening, added, "but there's an abortion that's just beginning. You could watch that."

Abortion? Somehow I had never considered the possibility of viewing an abortion! Since childhood I had attended church, and at an early age I committed myself to living by the principles God had set for me. I thought of myself as morally opposed to abortion in principle, but still something made it impossible for me to regard abortion as wrong in every instance.

Surely, I reasoned, there must be isolated instances where abortion is the best option. Simple curiosity, as well as my desire to be considered "open minded," overcame any doubts I had, and I hastily agreed to observe the procedure.

I paused briefly before the operating room door and squeezed my eyes shut. Then, composing myself, I slipped inside, where everything was in place and the procedure was about to begin.

The lights, the smells, the neat rows of instruments—it was all familiar. I reminded myself that this was a hospital operating room, not some back-alley "clinic," and that there was nothing sinister about it. This was possibly the very same operating room where I would have stood to watch the Caesarean birth.

From the foot of the operating table, I could see that the mother was already under the influence of the general anesthetic. She was about my age, and I began to fantasize about why she had decided on this abortion. Perhaps she'd been pressured by the father of the baby or by her parents. Maybe she was financially unable to care for a child, or perhaps it was just an inconvenient time for a pregnancy.

The low murmuring of the anesthesiologist, the O.R. nurse and the physician interrupted my thoughts. I then focused on the procedure itself. Dilators of increasing diameter were gradually inserted into the cervix, or neck, of the uterus until it was stretched enough to insert the suction tube.

I watched with interest—it was all so clinical, so normal, so much like other surgeries I'd previously observed. The medical personnel talked casually as they would during any procedure. My clenched fingers uncurled, and my rigid back muscles softened. I slowly relaxed and grew more comfortable.

The suction tube was connected to a bottle; inside the bottle a gauze bag dangled, waiting to catch the portions of tissue, which would be sent to the lab for routine examination after the procedure was completed.

When the suction machine was flipped on, its smooth whirring brought a flow of blood down the tube. Then I heard a soft "plop," and the physician muttered an obscenity as she realized that the gauze bag containing the tissue had somehow fallen into the blood at the bottom of the suction bottle.

In what seemed to be only minutes, the procedure was completed, the suction tube was removed and the patient was ready to be wheeled to the recovery room.

One final task remained—the physician had to retrieve the bag of tissue from the suction bottle and have it sent to the pathology department. To ease the task, the physician and the O.R. nurse decided to dump the contents of the bottle onto an instrument tray.

As the physician's gloved fingers poked through the blood, I looked again at the young, unconscious woman and wondered how she'd feel when she awoke. Relieved? Ashamed? Frightened?

My thoughts were interrupted by the physician. "Oooh, look," she whispered. "I've never seen one come out like this before. Here, take a look!"

I stepped closer, and she extended her bloody, gloved hand. Then I froze in horror as I saw what was cradled in her palm: a tiny body. This was not the "blob of tissue" that I expected to see after such an efficient, clinical procedure.

This was a fully formed, 12-week-old *decapitated* fetus. Two tiny arms with the smallest fingers imaginable hung from thin shoulders. Two fragile legs dangled from the delicate torso. About 2 1/2 to 3 inches in length, this was a perfect miniature human body.

"I'm sure the head is here, too," the O.R. nurse spoke in animated tones, still examining the tangled contents of the gauze snare.

Sick waves of revulsion churned in my stomach, and I backed toward the operating room door. I knew, beyond any doubt, that what I'd witnessed had been the taking of a human life and that there could be no possible justification for it.

When I reached the safety of the dressing room, I stepped clumsily out of the scrub dress and fumbled with the buttons on my uniform. I felt numb. Dry eyed, I sat down on the wooden bench and absently scuffed my feet together, noticing with interest that black lines now marred the shine on my white shoes. I'm not sure how many minutes passed before I mustered the strength to get up and walk to the maternity floor. The cries of newborn babies assaulted my ears, shrill and distorted. I stopped in front of the glass windows of the Special Care Nursery and gazed at the incredibly tiny infants, several of them barely four months older than the infant I'd just seen cradled in a bloody hand. Thousands of dollars were being spent to sustain their lives—why wasn't the life of that other infant just as important?

Two decades have passed since that spring day in Rochester, and I still like to think of myself as an "open-minded" person. But I'm absolutely certain of *this*: abortion involves the taking of human life. That small lifeless baby I gazed at, horrified, will never celebrate a birthday, walk in the park, smell the flowers or hear the birds. I've buried its memory for too long, and now I'm haunted by the thought of millions of tiny bodies being placed in specimen bottles and sent to pathology labs [32 million at last count].

I've asked God to forgive me for remaining silent, and to give me the courage to speak. He has, and in speaking I find a measure of peace. Now, at last, my tears flow freely, as I remember that day long ago when life was young and lilacs bloomed.

Kathy Schriefer is a nurse living in Pennsylvania.

Abortion: Pro-Life Versus Pro-Choice

Do you feel like David standing up to Goliath when defending your pro-life beliefs on abortion? The following statements are what pro-choice advocates use most often when arguing for abortion. How can *you* respond?

Put *these* answers in your slingshot when confronted with pro-choice ideas:

• *The fetus is just a part of the pregnant woman's body, like her tonsils or appendix.*

A fetus is NOT just another part of a woman's body. A body part is defined by the common genetic code it shares with the rest of the body. The unborn's genetic code differs from its mother's. Some of them are even male, while their moms are obviously female.

• *The unborn is a simple blob of tissue. So abortion is terminating a pregnancy, not killing a baby.*

An unborn human is NOT just a blob of tissue. From the moment of conception the unborn is what it is—a separate, LIVING human being.

• *The fetus is a potential human being, not an actual one; it's like a blueprint, not a house.*

A fetus is NOT just a blueprint or a "potential human." A fetus is a person at a particular state of development—much like a toddler or adolescent. The fact is, something nonhuman does not become human by getting older and bigger.

• *Life begins at birth. That's why we celebrate birthdays, not conception days.*

Life does NOT begin at birth. Science has shown us that human life begins at conception. All genetic characteristics of a distinct individual are present from the moment of conception. Our recognition of birthdays is cultural, not scientific.

• *Reproductive freedom is a basic right. Therefore, every woman should have control over her own body and have the right to choose.*

Restricting abortion does NOT step all over a woman's "rights and freedoms." If anything, it ensures the rights and freedoms of the unborn. The one-time choice of abortion robs someone else of a lifetime of choices. Furthermore, responsible societies *must* restrict choices that would harm others.

• *If abortion is made illegal, thousands of women will lose their lives to "rusty clothes hangers" in back alleys.*

Not true. Prior to its legalization, 90 percent of abortions were done by physicians in their offices, not in back alleys. In fact, women in America still die from *legal* abortions.

• *The unborn isn't a person with meaningful life. It can't even think and is less advanced than an animal.*

The early stages of human life *are* as meaningful as any other stage. But if we listened to pro-abortionists, who base human value on size and intelligence, we'd also have to dehumanize other members of society: dwarfs, basketball centers, the obese, the mentally handicapped and so on.

• *It's unfair to bring an unwanted child into this world. It'll probably end up being abused.*

A pregnancy may be "unwanted," but there is no such thing as an unwanted child. The list of couples wanting to adopt runs into the millions. And if we exclude all human beings who we believe are "unwanted," then *any* segment of society is at risk: AIDS victims, the elderly, derelicts and so on.

These statements were adapted from *Pro-Life Answers to Pro-Choice Arguments* by Randy C. Alcorn (Sisters, OR: Multnomah Books, 1992).

FOR FURTHER THOUGHT...

- How did you react to nurse Kathy Schriefer's story?
- What have you heard about abortion from friends or at school?
- What do these passages have to say about the unborn?

  Psalm 22:9,10

  Psalm 71:6

  Psalm 139:13-16

  Isaiah 44:2,24

  Isaiah 49:5

  Jeremiah 1:5

- Are your friends influencing your beliefs on abortion, or are you influencing theirs? Why do you answer the way you do?

????

We'd Rather Not Talk About It

We could sweep it aside and pretend it doesn't exist. We could say, "Go ask your parents or youth leader or pastor or school counselor." We could advise you to send a letter to a magazine—anonymously—and *hope* they write back or publish an answer six to eight months later. We could even say, "Good Christians don't ever think about something so perverse!" That would end the discussion, but it wouldn't end the "weird feelings" a few have toward the same sex. Nor would it answer honest questions that might occasionally pop into your head.

Frankly, we know this is a BIG issue with a SMALL percentage of teens, but we care about you too much to not talk about homosexuality as honestly as possible. We've never practiced, thought about or even dabbled with this sexual dilemma, so we talked to someone who has. This person has since become a Christian, rejected that lifestyle and even married.

WAS THERE ANYTHING IN YOUR GROWING UP YEARS THAT POSSIBLY CONTRIBUTED TO YOUR INVOLVEMENT IN THE HOMOSEXUAL LIFESTYLE?

My first memory of being attracted to guys was in grade school when I found "normal-type, straight" pornography on the side of the road. Later, I happened upon it at home—my father had a problem with it. Eventually, my parents caught me with it a few times. Instead of talking to me about it, however, I was told it was "unnatural." Or, "I'm disappointed with you. Go to your room."

Another factor was my dad. He was a hothead, and he didn't know how to say, "I love you," hug me or give me any affection. I found out later there were two reasons for that: First, when he was a child, he was molested by men. Second, he didn't have a dad to show *him* how to be a dad, so he thought giving affection to his son would be perverse.

Though I didn't have the strong father figure that guys need, I don't believe it *caused* the way I turned out. But I do think my weaknesses were related to my dad's past.

Then, when I was 12, I was molested by a neighbor who wanted to show me some homosexual videos. I didn't deserve or want the molestation, but I *did* want to see the movies. That opened the door to lots of thoughts and ideas during my junior high and high school years. To be honest, I didn't know what was wrong with me or what was happening.

The pornography helped me act out fantasies in my mind. I was also a habitual masturbator. I'd do it several times a day. Once my mom caught me, but there was no discussion. Inside I knew I needed help. I wish my parents would have talked to me.

I realized later that you have two choices: you either get help, or you go into what you've fed on and struggled with for years.

WHAT WAS GOING THROUGH YOUR MIND DURING YOUR TEEN YEARS WHEN YOU STRUGGLED WITH THOSE THOUGHTS AND FEELINGS?

There's a verse that says, "As he thinks in his heart, so is he" (Prov. 23:7, NKJV). Most of my life I hated myself because I thought I was different or weird. I heard my parents say, "Homosexuals are gross, awful, and perverted." I was thinking, *I don't act like the homosexuals I see on TV. And I'm not effeminate like them, but I have those feelings. Therefore, I must be gross, awful, perverse—and homosexual.*

Another problem I had—probably related to my own father—was I didn't develop healthy male-to-male friendships. I had friends, but I felt weird around them. I was more comfortable around girls. I didn't fit in with the guys.

My sophomore year in college, I tried to kill myself because I thought I was going crazy. I prayed, "God, if my feelings are wrong, take me." I wrote a note, and that night I slept with a knife. Several times throughout the night I held it to my throat or wrists. What prevented me from following through was I didn't want to end up hurting myself and surviving. Later, when those suicidal thoughts returned, I'd just break down and cry at night, seeing myself in a casket and knowing my parents would be devastated.

It's very selfish to think of killing yourself. You're done with life, but everyone else has to suffer and have the pain of losing you. People think they're going to run away from their problems, but the instant you die, you're going to face God. That could be a BIG problem!

DID YOU HAVE A CHRISTIAN UPBRINGING?

My parents were semichurch goers, but in their minds it became too social. I do remember hearing about Jesus in Sunday School, though. Then when I was a teen, I went on weekend trips with Young Life where I heard even more about Jesus. I probably asked Christ to come into my heart over 100 times, but my homosexual thoughts never quit or stopped. Again, I wanted to talk to someone, but the leaders in that particular group and in my church hung out with the cool and popular guys. I wasn't funny or fun or popular; I was just a normal kid.

Before you entered that lifestyle, did you try anything else to stay straight?

I dated and slept with girls to see if I was normal and to try to prove to myself and others that I was straight. One girl wanted to marry me. She was a beautiful model-type. She kept my mind off the thoughts, but I still knew I couldn't marry her because I had to see if I was a homosexual.

At age 21, I finally decided it was time to find out if I was. I drove to downtown areas where I'd heard there were gay bars. About my third time there, I met my first male sexual partner. By then I had so much bottled up, I *flew* out of the closet. There was no remorse, no guilt, no nothing.

What did you do with your conscience while you were actively practicing homosexuality?

I said, "God, I'm going to do what I want." Drugs and alcohol helped me bury my conscience. While I temporarily felt better, my usage eventually led to harder drugs.

Even though I stayed in the closet for a long time, crying, "God, change me," He didn't change me. The reason was, I didn't want to change. I wanted my sin. A verse says, "But each one is tempted when, by his own evil desire, he is dragged away and enticed" (Jas. 1:14). Though I prayed and cried, I also wanted the sin.

The first time I felt guilt was when a guy came up off the street and said, "You've been deceived and you'll deceive others." He wasn't a street preacher and he didn't have a Bible—perhaps he was an angel. Anyway, I went to church twice after that, and the pastor talked about that very mes-

225 WE'D RATHER NOT TALK ABOUT IT 225

sage. I knew it was from God, and I knew I couldn't handle it. I thought I had finally found myself, so I said, "I ain't going to go back in that closet God, so, good-bye."

For five years I led a pretty ugly and fast-paced lifestyle. About three years into it, I got weary. I wondered if I'd ever find that love of my life. Much of the homosexual community is a back-stabbing, dog-eat-dog type of world. In those five years, I had nearly 150 partners. That's probably low for some homosexuals. I wanted a committed relationship, but that's extremely rare, especially among younger homosexual men.

When I got hurt by someone, I decided it wouldn't happen to me again. I became like the people I hated and wound up hurting others like I had been hurt. People who start out in that lifestyle think it's going to work. But relationships don't last for more than a few months, if even that long. Then I'd get tired of that person and would be ready to move on. Even while I was dating someone, I was looking around.

How do guys get into it?

I don't believe there is any *one* reason people go into homosexuality. Many of the guys I knew were molested by an uncle or a neighbor or someone. That's how the door is sometimes opened. And *all* of them were affected by pornography. Also, you have to look at the sins of the father. Many have fathers who were not home, and others stayed emotionally distant because of something hurtful that may have happened to them.

Guys move from wanting to see homosexual pictures or videos to wanting to try it with a real person. After a while, pornography just doesn't seem to be enough.

How do girls first get involved?

Again, there's not one specific answer. Many of the girls I knew who were lesbians were molested by men. They learned to be disgusted with them because of the way they were treated. They entered homosexuality to get their emotional needs met and thought another woman could do that better than a male. Many had a very bad relationship with their moms, which made me wonder if they were trying to fill that void with another woman.

It seems like it takes a woman longer to come out of the lesbian lifestyle. They're more committed to making it work, and they're not confronted with lovers they've known who are dying from AIDS as much as men are.

HOW DO CHRISTIANS STRUGGLE WITH THIS? CAN'T THEY JUST REJECT IT AND BECOME STRAIGHT?

Christians *do* struggle with this. For me, Jesus was my Savior, but not my Lord. I hadn't given Him *all* of my life; I'd only given Him *parts*. Romans 7 talks about a man's flesh desiring something, while his spirit hates it. I think that's the battle Christians face. It becomes *very* hard to just reject it and move on. God will often have to break them before they give it up. That's the way it was with me.

But if someone is full-out into the lifestyle, that's between God and him. I knew where I was: no-man's-land. I didn't know if I would have gone to heaven if I died. Because Jesus said, "If you love me, you will obey what I command" (John 14:15). When you're in that type of dilemma, there's probably reason to doubt that Christ is really in your life.

I knew the truth, but the truth hadn't set me free (see John 8:32).

WHAT ABOUT THE ARGUMENT YOU HEAR IN THE NEWSPAPERS THAT BEING A HOMOSEXUAL IS DETERMINED AT BIRTH?

I've heard those reports wouldn't stand up scientifically. I've read some of those reports, but they look like they were done to try to prove a point. From what I've seen, I'd say that being attracted to the same sex isn't a chromosomal thing, but a spiritual thing.

It's just like a car wreck you didn't cause. If you're hit from the back and it's not your fault, you still have to take care of it (deal with the insurance, call the cops, take your car in for repairs). People may be born with weaknesses or tendencies (like being in a car wreck), but they are still responsible for how they deal with those feelings. They make the choices to feed and act on their thoughts. *God doesn't cause someone to be a homosexual.* We're in a fallen world so people make wrong choices—even though they know better.

YOU ESCAPED THAT LIFE. WHAT HAPPENED?

First of all, I knew I was HIV positive about a year before I changed. It was then I started planning my death. Everyone I knew had so many friends dying of AIDS that all they wanted to do was party until they died. And that's the way I felt. But God had other ideas. It's been over six years since I came back to Christ. Though I know I may die before my time because of the lifestyle I chose, I'm not mad at God. Plus, I have a wife who loves me and understands the situation I'm in, and that's more than I ever dreamed possible.

When I gave up that lifestyle years ago, I lost all of my homosexual friends. I don't blame them. Even the Bible says, "What fellowship can light have with darkness?" (2 Cor. 6:14). When they were doing drugs and I didn't anymore, they felt uncomfortable around me.

It was at this time I wished I would have known there were ex-gay ministries. When a homosexual friend and I really committed our lives to Christ, we thought we were the only two to ever change. Then we saw the Scripture, "Do you not know that the wicked will not inherit the kingdom of God? Do not be deceived: Neither the sexually immoral nor idolaters nor adulterers nor male prostitutes *nor homosexual offenders* nor thieves nor the greedy nor drunkards nor slanderers nor swindlers will inherit the kingdom of God. *And that is what some of you were.* But you were washed, you were sanctified, you were justified in the name of the Lord Jesus Christ and by the Spirit of our God" (1 Cor. 6:9-11, italics added). We finally knew that even during Bible times Christians had come out of this lifestyle.

DO YOU STILL STRUGGLE WITH THOSE OLD FEELINGS, EVEN THOUGH YOU'RE NOW MARRIED?

If you take a bottle of whiskey and empty it, it still smells like whiskey. If you rinse it with water and empty it, it still smells. Even if you do that 50 times, you can still smell it. But the more I allow the Holy Spirit to rinse me out, I begin to smell less and less like I did before. I've gotten better, but the proverb can be true: "As a dog returns to its vomit, so a fool repeats his folly" (Prov. 26:11). I've wanted to sip; to feel the comfort of what I knew. But things *have* changed. I have a stronger desire and more love for my wife. I also have a support system. I have people who say, "How are you really doing? Do you have anything you need to throw away?" Ex-homosexuals know when we're being honest with ourselves and others, and when we're trying to hide things. I say the same to others. I suppose I could deceive these friends, but then the Holy Spirit would give me a whippin'. God's not going to let go of me again that easy, and I truly love the life I now have with my wife.

HOW DO YOU REACH A HOMOSEXUAL? WHAT SHOULD CHRISTIANS DO TO HELP?

When people—homosexual or not—want to love their sin and stay there, that's when they're the toughest to reach. For me, it was a process of working out my salvation with fear and trembling; of renewing my mind daily. I had to get into God's Word every day, as well as find healthy same-sex friendships. You can't respond to the truth unless you know it to be true. And I couldn't trust God with my life until I really knew Him and how much He cared.

Christians should be the ones to help carry the weak or wounded until they can walk on their own. Unfortunately, with this problem, I don't see a lot of that happening—though it is getting better. Christians don't always respond right because they either don't know how, are afraid or they don't care. But if someone with homosexual leanings is reading this, there ARE Christians who care and do know how to help. They know how to love you through this to true freedom. Please find them and don't stay quiet. God will meet you in your struggle and help you live a life that brings true peace. I promise.

THIS ISN'T THE LAST WORD

A short interview with an ex-homosexual won't likely pull someone completely out who's already in too far. But, instead of just giving you a few Scripture references or facts, we thought this would give you a clearer picture of how this happens. Hundreds of cities in North America have an ex-homosexual ministry. Here is a ministry you can write to or call to start the process of getting healed— they know of ministries in nearly every city in America: Exodus International, P.O. Box 2121, San Rafael, CA 94912. (415) 454-1017.

FOR FURTHER THOUGHT...

• The world's perspective on homosexuality is vastly different from God's. What did you learn about homosexuality from this chapter?

• What did this chapter teach you about your attitude toward homosexuality? About the attitude God wants you to have?

• What did this chapter teach you about God?

????

Planning Your Honeymoon

Let's admit it. We've all dreamed about our honeymoon. (Well, maybe girls more than guys). The perfect place. The person we love more than anyone else in the whole world. No curfews. No physical limitations. Just love and paradise.

What would your perfect dream escape be?

A. Snowcapped mountains and a log cabin right next to a ski resort.
B. A sunny, white-sanded beach with lots of extras: parasailing, scuba diving, snorkeling, hang gliding, windsurfing.
C. The plush Disneyland hotel with a three-day pass to the Magic Kingdom.
D. A romantic New England resort with a big heart-shaped bathtub in your suite.
E. An exclusive getaway in a private Victorian mansion.
F. Camping along the river and riding rapids during the day.

We're almost done with the book, so we thought it would be good to not only review a few things we've covered so far, but also to ask you what is your personal fantasy. After all, it's not too early to start planning your honeymoon *now*.

What're ya talking about? I'm still in high school!

I know. But there's a LOT more to a honeymoon than simply choosing a place to go.

Yeah, like coming up with the cash for it!

Money is *one* thing, but there's more, too!

Like what?

Like preparing yourself *now* for your future mate. In other words, don't start the honeymoon too early. Remember, you can fall in and out of love several times with many people before you actually get married. And when you're in a relationship with someone you love—or even reallyreallyreally like—it's tempting to start the honeymoon early.
DON'T.
Save it *all* for that special night with your lifelong companion.

Yeah, yeah, yeah. I know what you're saying. And you've said it a million different ways so far in this book: Save yourself for marriage. But, I gotta be honest. I wanna get to know my partner's body.

Then you're starting the honeymoon too early. Do you want someone else exploring and getting to know your future mate's body? Because right now he/she is probably in a dating relationship. So treat *your* date the same way you want someone else to treat your future spouse.

Well, I'm in love with the person I'm dating. I'm sure we're going to get married, anyway.

Then save the exploring for your honeymoon. Think of it this way: A honeymoon shouldn't be two professionals coming together for a practiced love match. A honeymoon should be two amateurs figuring it out *together*. Learning *together*. Exploring *together*.

Your honeymoon will also be a lot more than sex. It's smelling bad breath and feeling someone's cold feet against yours. It's also waking up to see a bunch of sleepy gook oozing out of the edge of your partner's eyes and hearing funny noises from your new spouse when he/she's in the other room.

So how can I prepare for those things now?

By learning to be patient with people, not demanding your own way, becoming more flexible, placing other people's needs before your own.

OK, what else can I do to start preparing for my honeymoon now?

As Greg mentioned early on, learn the art of good conversation. A great honeymoon isn't simply "no holds barred" for a week; it's really communicating in an intimate way with your new mate.

So begin learning how to be a good communicator *now*. Ask questions that demand more than a yes/no answer. Learn how to be open and transparent. This will allow vulnerability, which, in turn, develops trust.

Is that it?

One more thing. And this is kind of basic. Determine to have really good solid friendships with the opposite sex. The kind of friendships you establish will determine the kind of dating relationships you have. And, more than likely, your marriage will be a reflection of your dating relationships.

Simply put: Good opposite sex friendships = good dating relationships = a good marriage.

And a good honeymoon? Well, that can set the tone for a great first year of marriage. So though you want to be careful not to *start* the honeymoon too early, start *becoming* the person your mate will want on the honeymoon—*now*.

Bonus Scoop: Take a few minutes *right now* to pray for your future husband/wife. Pray for God's protection on him/her. Pray for his/her relationship with Christ. Pray that he/she won't compromise. And ask God to help him/her begin the process *now* of becoming the future spouse you'll need, and don't forget to pray that *you'll* become the future mate *your* spouse needs.

FOR FURTHER THOUGHT...

- Have you thought about what you want your honeymoon to be like? Jot down some details.
- Do you think it's helpful to imagine yourself in the future? Why? Or why not?
- What do you hope God is doing in the life of your future mate right now?
- What are three specific things you can do now to be the husband/wife your spouse will need?
- What are some safeguards you can establish to make sure you don't start your honeymoon too early?

????

Divorce-Proofing Your Life

Most guys and girls your age will say with absolute certainty, "We'll never divorce." Yet statistics reveal that 50 percent of all marriages end in divorce. Though the stats are lower for Christian couples, many Christian families are still ripped apart by this disease of selfishness. I (Greg) didn't come from a Christian family, and I believe that's why my family was ripped apart. We had no foundation to stand on. I know first-hand the pain divorce can bring. You see, both of my parents were married three times before I was out of high school. Those painful memories are still vivid.

How can you avoid putting your future children through the agonies of divorce?

We've said a lot in this book, but we want to tie some loose ends together and reiterate a few things we've already mentioned. The reason? More than anything, we want you to have a lifetime of success with the opposite sex.

WHERE IT STARTS

When you were younger, you were given about a dozen shots so you'd never contract diseases such as tuberculosis, measles, polio, small pox, asparagusitis and so on. These shots kept you alive and well by giving you the immunities necessary to fight off the disease, should you ever come in contact with it.

The only way to avoid divorce is through preventative medicine. When should you start taking it? During marriage? Courtship? College?

Actually, the time to start is right now! The symptoms that lead to the disease of divorce could get a chance to grow if they aren't "immunized" today.

When you were little, you didn't have a choice—you were forced to get shots so you'd stay alive (no doubt sometimes crying and screaming). But today you have a choice whether you'll divorce-proof your life or not. The choice occurs in how you view the opposite sex.

DIVORCE-PROOF "SHOTS" FOR GUYS

"SHOT" NUMBER ONE

The number-one preventable disease that leads to divorce is *what you choose to set your eyes on—namely, pornography.* What goes through your eyes goes into your brain. If your mind can be educated to pick up algebra, it can be trained to believe lies about the opposite sex.

Without embarrassing or condemning every guy out there, let's admit a few things:

1. As we said, stumbling onto pornography usually happens accidentally. A friend at school will bring some pictures he found or got from his older brother, or perhaps you'll see it on the side of the road, or you'll notice it at the corner convenience store—it's everywhere. It's a multibillion-dollar-a-year industry with this strategy: hook younger guys on it so they'll buy it the rest of their lives. If pornogra-

phers can satisfy a natural curiosity early in life, guys will be captured by it and purchase it on a regular basis.

2. What do guys "buy" when they become obsessed with their natural curiosity about the female anatomy? Like any drug or alcoholic beverage, pornography is addictive. Looking at it releases a chemical in the brain that initially brings pleasure. The more a guy exposes his mind to those images, however, the more he wants to see. He's hooked.

Though the pictures seem to promise unlimited sexual freedom, what they deliver is frustration, guilt and an *extremely dangerous* message that girls are objects to be used.

3. A steady diet of pornography from now until age 23, when most guys get married, totally warps a guy's ability to look at a female as someone to be respected, loved and nurtured. Instead, girls are viewed as something from which to get pleasure by meeting a guy's "needs." This isn't anywhere near God's purpose for females.

4. You don't have to be a professional counselor to realize that a woman won't want to live too long with a guy who treats her like an object.

5. Girls who pose for magazines are making money. Photographers are making money. Advertisers are making money. The stores are making money. And organized crime is making *a lot* of money.

6. You can't pick up a Bible without reading how valuable and special people are to God. It was never His intention that people devalue themselves for money and pleasure.

"SHOT" NUMBER TWO

TV, movies, magazines and billboards have also taught us guys to use a rating system—usually based on facial appearance and body curves. Every guy is affected by this barrage of false information.

We've learned to judge a girl's value based on what Hollywood or the advertising world tells us is beautiful. Though it's too ingrained in our society to get rid of, it doesn't have to mess up our heads forever.

First, admit the fact that you probably rate girls by an unfair standard. Go ahead, nod your head up and down. (There, that wasn't so tough.)

Second, commit yourself to never verbally rate another girl in front of other people. Statements such as, "She's a dog—better make sure your shots are up-to-date," "She's an ultra-10 to the ultimate maximum," or "Put a bag over her head and she'd be fine" don't exactly fit with the idea that everyone is incredibly important to God.

Though not many guys would have the guts to speak up if a friend said stuff like that, try not to encourage him by laughing or agreeing.

Why such a hard slap at a rating system that's practically second nature?

Simple. Your future happiness with the girl God gives you to spend the rest of your life with is dependent on it.

If you aggressively practice rating girls for 10 or so years before marriage, the habit won't be broken just because you go through a ceremony. Your mind is trained to rate every girl on false standards.

After the honeymoon feelings wear off, men sometimes begin to think they could find something better. If a man has a wife who is a 7 and someone is available close by who is a 9 or 10, many guys would make some *very wrong* choices. Divorce is the result. It's called the "greener pasture" syndrome.

A rating system firmly entrenched in the mind of a guy will cause him to always think he could've done better. (If any girls are reading this, please don't think this is just a problem guys have! Your turn is coming!) Does this mean you shouldn't try to find fine-looking girls to spend

time with during the teenage years? No. As we've said already, it simply means there's more to females than what you see.

Practice looking beyond the outside and find out about their personality, their likes and dislikes, and especially see if their taste in fast foods matches yours! If they're into Taco Bell and you're a Wendy's fanatic, you're in for a loser of a relationship. (Just kidding, sort of.)

"SHOT" NUMBER THREE

The last thing to help divorce-proof your life is working on a minor little selfishness problem guys have.

Actually, it's not so minor, and selfishness is a kind way to put it. Let's be honest: Using another person to gratify your pleasures is sin.

There—that ugly little three-letter word—we said it.

A natural result of pornography, Hollywood and the rating system guys have bought into is the belief that girls were put on earth to make them feel good. Therefore, the belief goes, when a guy finds a girl to spend time with, she ought to make herself available for him to explore.

Are there sexual limits? Yes, but there are problems for the guy who wants to stick by them.

Guys have three facts to contend with: (1) Fueled by the media's obsession with sex, teenage hormones tend to race at a higher pace younger in life; (2) More females are agreeing with the conclusion that they *should* be available for guys to explore; (3) With all of the "education" in school on safe sex, it would be easy to believe there are no limits in the playground of physical involvement—as long as you're "protected." In essence, the public school system teaches you how to sin—intelligently.

If you're a Christian, you probably know what the limits are. They're usually heard from two sources: (1) Christian adults who seem scared to death that teens are growing up, (2) a big book with a ton of words and not too many pictures called the Bible.

Stay with me on this one for a second 'cause it's kind of a big issue.

No matter how impossible it seems, imagine this: Imagine that the adults in your life really care about you. (Hopefully, that's not too hard to imagine!) Your parents, youth leader, pastor—all these folks—genuinely love you and 100 percent want you to have a great life. Their voices likely try to convince you to save yourself for one person.

Now, imagine this truth: God wants your life to be even better than these adults do! Because He created you, allowed His Son, Jesus, to die on a cross to take away the penalty of your sin, knows your future, knows your mind (and loves you anyway!) and knows when you'll get your next zit—please believe that He knows what He's talking about when it comes to sex.

Remember in chapter 19 when we talked about your dilemma and God's dilemma? Tell me: If you're God, are you going to shower down incredible gifts on these people if they make the right choices or what?

That's what God wants to do with the gift of sex for men and women who obey the guidelines He's given in His Word.

Daily, we face the dilemma of other voices screaming for our thought time. The temptation to give in to them is incredible. Obeying these voices destroys one of God's most precious gifts—the intimacy and purity between a man and a woman.

Trying to get all you can from girls during the teenage years convinces you of the lie that females are only designed to meet your physical needs. It also stains your mind with images of other girls once you've chosen to marry. You end up constantly comparing one girl to another. It totally robs a guy of the purity and closeness he really wants in a lifetime companion.

Divorce-Proof "Shots" For Girls

"Shot" Number One

Picture a bustling city street. Your job is to stand on the corner and ask every woman passing by between the ages of 12 and 21 this question: *Did you ever believe that if you just had a boyfriend you'd be happy?*

If you stopped 100 girls, every one of them would probably say yes. Here's why:

• Moms and daughters talk about their wedding day—a lot.

• If you watch soap operas on TV, the only time the female stars are happy is when they have the guys they want.

• Romance novels feed on the female preoccupation with finding Mr. Right.

• Barbie has Ken. Cinderella and Snow White have their princes. The Little Mermaid has her dream of being with a human guy. And Beauty has the Beast.

• Pop radio is filled with "love songs."

• Girls' magazines constantly talk about "how to get him to like you."

It's impossible for girls not to think that the pot of gold at the end of their rainbow is a guy.

Yes, God has something to do with it, too. He has placed the desire for a guy inside every girl. But nowhere does He say, *"As soon as you find a guy, you'll know that My blessing is upon you and you'll be happy forever."* There's a reason God is silent.

He knows the happiest day of your life will be the day you realize this: NO GUY ON THIS PLANET WILL MEET ALL YOUR NEEDS. That role is played by only ONE—Jesus Christ.

Let's go back to the street to prove it. Now you're asking women *over* the age of 25 the same question. Nearly all would say they learned a long time ago that a man can't make them happy. *Hmmmm.* Do you think they know something you don't?

Girls want boyfriends for a number of reasons—some good, some bad:

1. It's normal, and guys CAN BE fun to be with. (Good point.)

2. If they have a popular boyfriend, then they'll be popular, too. (Very true, but also very selfish. In essence, they're using the guy to get some social needs met. This happens all the time, and it's a pretty lame thing to do. Unfortunately, guys do the same.)

3. They need someone to love them. If someone loves you—especially a guy—it makes you feel important, special

and worthwhile. (This is probably the number one reason why girls are unhappy. This is God's job, remember! Not a guy's!)

4. They want someone to love. (Not a bad reason, except they forget one thing: most teenage guys equate love with sex. That is, love is something to be *proved*, not shared. Nearly all teenage guys have no clue what genuine love really is.)

If a girl or a guy goes into a relationship (or a marriage), thinking that the other will make them happy, that relationship (or marriage) won't make it. Jesus said, "The thief comes only to steal and kill and destroy; I have come that they may have life, and have it to the full" (John 10:10). Don't transfer to another person the responsibility for your happiness when only One ever promised He could give it to you.

The second commandment fits perfectly: "You shall have no other gods before me" (Exod. 20:3). Unfortunately, that's what guys and girls have done. They've made the opposite sex their god. The real God who made you knows this, and weeps.

"Shot" Number Two

We talked earlier about how guys rate girls—how dangerous a habit it is to get into. Girls don't just rate guys; they have perfected it into a game. We call it "Rating Pursuit."

The object is to move up the ladder by "going with" the most popular guy available. If a girl is spending time with someone she considers a 6, she'll drop him fast if an 8 starts showing interest in her.

Why? Correct me if I'm wrong, Susie, but girls (like a lot of guys) are insecure. That is, they're not totally comfortable with just being themselves. If they have a group, or a boyfriend to whom they can attach themselves, it makes them feel better about themselves.

There's no guarantee that if a girl plays the "Rating Pursuit" game until she gets married, she won't continue rating other guys after marriage. (*I agree —Susie*)

"SHOT" NUMBER THREE

Some girls will do anything to get a popular boyfriend, but then they make an even more fatal mistake—THEY DO ANYTHING TO KEEP HIM. Many will allow a guy to go exploring. Some will even give away their sexual purity in hopes they'll stay together.

It's becoming more common for teenage girls to have had sex with more than one guy before she decides whom to marry. (It's even more common among guys.) God forgives these mistakes to all who ask for it, but our own conscience isn't so forgiving. A computer chip in our brain has stored the experience for future reference. After each successive sexual mistake, comparisons between them all come to the surface.

Finally, when she's chosen one guy for the rest of her life, those memories won't leave her alone. She'll never be able to look at her man without thinking of others she's had as well. In the search for short-term attention and popularity, many give away a lifetime of intimacy—the very thing they really want AND the very thing God wants to give.

That's why physical involvement is such a tragedy for both guys and girls. God promises a lifetime of sharing, surprises, struggles and intimacy. Instead, it's traded in for something as shallow as popularity and a false sense of love.

WHAT DO YOU WANT?

I know this final chapter seemed more like a sermon, but we know that handling the guy/girl thing right during the high school years is essential for a lifetime of real success with the opposite sex. Each year, both of us receive hundreds of letters from *Brio* and *Breakaway* readers that tell us the mistakes they've made—and what it has cost them. It's sad. We shed real tears. It doesn't need to be like that! we want to scream.

We hope this book has given you the ideas, ammunition and encouragement you need to be a REAL success with the opposite sex.

Discussion Leader's Guide

A WORD TO LEADERS

Don't you wish you would have had *What Hollywood Won't Tell You About Sex, Love and Dating* when you were in high school? That is the reaction of many adults who have read this book, and it underscores the exciting opportunity this book gives you to share a Christian perspective on love, on sex and on dating, a perspective that can help young people today avoid some of the mistakes others have made and are making.

So how can you make the best of this opportunity? Here are some tips!

THE MATERIAL: DIVIDE AND CONQUER!

Don't let the table of contents throw you! The 31 chapters in the book don't mean 31 weeks of discussion! You can approach this material in a lot of ways. Choose the one that best fits the time you have, the points you want to emphasize and—most important—the kids in your group.

- **A Standard 13-Week Study**—In Week 1, focus on the introductory Part I. Then spend three weeks on each of the next four parts. Here is one schedule:
  Weeks 2, 3 and 4: chapters 4-7, 8, 9 and 10, 11, respectively;
  Weeks 5, 6 and 7: chapters 12, 13 and 14;
  Weeks 8, 9 and 10: chapters 15-17, 18-20 and 21-24;
  Weeks 11, 12 and 13: chapters 25, 26, 27-29 and 30, 31.

- **A Mini 4-Week Study**—If you know your kids, you know what they have heard a hundred times and you know the issues they are facing daily on campus. Choose two or three chapters for each of the four group times, ideally pulling from all five parts of the book.

- **A Weekend Retreat**—Before you pack your duffel bags, have the kids submit questions (anonymously). What do they want to know about—but are afraid to ask? Have them choose topics from the list of chapter titles you give them—and they don't necessarily need to know these are chapter titles. It will sure help you prepare, though!

However long you plan to spend on *What Hollywood Won't Tell You About Sex, Love and Dating*, you might want to inform parents about what you will be discussing. No one likes to be surprised by hard questions that might be raised at home as a result of some of the issues you discuss.

Now take some time to consider how you will pace your discussions. A lot depends on whether you are meeting for an hour or two hours! Keep in mind, however, that we all need variety. Very few of us—especially when we are in high school—do well, listening to a straight lecture for an extended period of time.

— When can you break up large-group time by having two or three people talk together among themselves?

— When can you have someone else take the lead?

— Where can you use a high schooler to guide the group through some of the questions?

— How will you open your time together? Do you have a repertoire of nonthreatening, ice-breaker questions?

— And how will you close your time? Will you pray? Will you make time for the guys and girls to pray?

There is no right or wrong way to lead your group. Do what feels right. Learn from what works and what doesn't.

THE GUYS AND THE GIRLS: EDUCATE AND ENCOURAGE

As important as knowing your material is, knowing your kids is even more important. And as much as you will want a polished presentation that God can use to touch hearts and give the young people in your group the strength to save sex for marriage, even more important is modeling openness and honesty with them so that they will be comfortable with you in the group and comfortable enough to go to you later if they want to.

Know that the tone of the discussion will be set largely by you! If you are uptight (whether it is about your car that is in the shop or the deadline at work), your group will be tense, too. But if you are comfortable talking about God's wonderful and mysterious gift of sex, you will be able to help the guys and girls in your group relax.

If you are judgmental and puritanical and come across as a mistrusting parent, don't expect free and open discussions. But if you have made mistakes that you are willing to share (think ahead about what you want to share and how you will do that), you will be giving the young people in the group permission to be human—to admit their mistakes, confess their sins and receive Christ's forgiveness.

Most of all, if you genuinely love the guys and the girls in the group and truly want them to understand the precious gift God has given to us humans by making us sexual beings, your love will encourage those in your group to risk, to learn, to grow, to confess, to repent and to decide to save that gift for the person they marry.

THE GROUP: MAKING IT WORK

Some group dynamics are basic to any group, any age, any topic. But what you have here is a real hot topic and a real volatile, sensitive, curious, I-know-it-all, I-want-to-be-accepted, let's-be-cool (you remember adolescence!) age. How can you make your group work?

- Explain the ground rules on Day 1 and reiterate them from time to time as you see fit.

   — No one has to talk. You are not getting graded!

   — But those who do, have to give others the chance to talk! No hogging all our discussion time!

   — Let's stay on track! I know you all have stories to tell about people you know and lessons you have learned—but we don't have all year!

   — Be kind! Do unto others! Give people a break! Not everyone is as clued in as you are. Not everyone has all the answers that you have. So cut out the laughing and nervous giggling. Do your best imitation of an adult!

— If you have a question, someone else probably
has that same question. But if you don't feel like
sharing it in the group, write it down, put it in
this box and I will answer it next time! (Be sure
to have the box, check for questions, and
answer those you find!)

— Everything that is said is to be confidential!
That means everything—and that means no
telling, not even to your best friend!

• Directing questions to specific people—but only to
those you know can handle it—is one way to quiet a
dominator. Be careful not to call on someone who
will be mortified to be forced to speak!

• As you've seen in the text, some chapters are just for
girls and some just for the guys. Let these guidelines
guide your group. Divide into two groups for these
discussions and then come back together.

• Be prepared! Choose which "For Further Thought"
questions (found at the end of each chapter) you
want to address. Try to anticipate questions that may
come up and have answers ready. As mentioned earlier, think through what you want to share about
your own mistakes along the way and how you will
do that. If you are tackling the book over an extended period of time, consider guest speakers (experts
on certain aspects of sexuality and relationships or a
young person whose testimony may carry some
weight with the group).

• Be sensitive to your audience. Pay attention to how
the discussion seems to be affecting members of the
group. Note who might need some time with you or
another leader outside the group.

• Last—and by far the most important—pray! Pray for
your group. Pray for your time together. Pray for the

kids individually. Ask God to give them ears to hear those points they need most right now and to sow His seeds so they will have the truth and the strength they will need later on.

May God bless you as you lead some very special young people through *What Hollywood Won't Tell You About Sex, Love and Dating.*

Okay, What's Next?!

Here's God's Plan for Success with the Opposite Sex.
Success with the opposite sex depends on self respect and following God's plan. This book will help 5th through 9th graders counteract the pressure to grow up too fast.

Getting Ready for the Guy/Girl Thing
By Greg Johnson and Susie Shellenberger
Paperback • ISBN 08307.14855

See Yourself in a Whole New Light.
Here is the powerful message of Neil Anderson's best-selling book Victory over the Darkness written especially for young people. Stomping Out the Darkness provides you with keys to your identity, worth, significance, security and acceptance as a child of God.

Stomping Out the Darkness
By Neil T. Anderson and Dave Park
Paperback • ISBN 08307.16408

A Fun Way to Solve Life's Puzzles.
A fun and simple way to understand the basics of Christianity. It's a 32-page comic book size evangelism tool filled with games, puzzles and more.

So, What's a Christian Anyway?
Paperback • ISBN 08307.13972

A Mazing Way to Walk with the Lord.
Here's a fun way to discover how to put your faith into action—cleverly disguised as a comic book. Includes dozens of games, puzzles and mazes interwoven with daily Scripture readings and rock-solid teaching.

Yo! I'm a Christian, Now What?
Paperback • ISBN 08307.14669

These books are available at your local Christian bookstore.

Gospel Light